NEW HAVEN FREE PUBLIC LIBRARY

3 5000 07485 6062

P9-CEB-356

For Reference
Do Not Take
From the Library

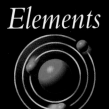

Elements

SULFUR

S

FREE PUBLIC LIBRARY
133 ELM ST
NEW HAVEN CT 06510

 Grolier Educational

SHERMAN TURNPIKE, DANBURY, CONNECTICUT 06816

How to use this book

This book has been carefully developed to help you understand the chemistry of the elements. In it you will find a systematic and comprehensive coverage of the basic qualities of each element. Each two-page entry contains information at various levels of technical content and language, along with definitions of useful technical terms, as shown in the thumbnail diagram to the right. There is a comprehensive glossary of technical terms at the back of the book, along with an extensive index, key facts, an explanation of the periodic table, and a description of how to interpret chemical equations.

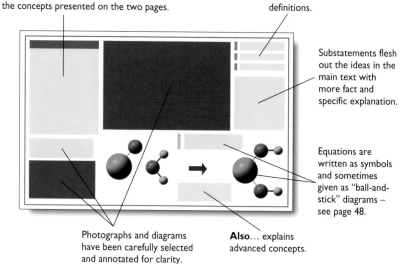

The main text follows the sequence of information in the book and summarizes the concepts presented on the two pages.

Technical definitions.

Substatements flesh out the ideas in the main text with more fact and specific explanation.

Equations are written as symbols and sometimes given as "ball-and-stick" diagrams – see page 48.

Photographs and diagrams have been carefully selected and annotated for clarity.

Also… explains advanced concepts.

Author
Brian Knapp, BSc, PhD
Project consultant
Keith B. Walshaw, MA, BSc, DPhil
        (Head of Chemistry, Leighton Park School)
Industrial consultant
Jack Brettle, BSc, PhD (Chief Research Scientist, Pilkington plc)
Art Director
Duncan McCrae, BSc
Editor
Elizabeth Walker, BA
Special photography
Ian Gledhill
Illustrations
David Woodroffe and David Hardy
Designed and produced by
EARTHSCAPE EDITIONS
Print consultants
Landmark Production Consultants Ltd
Reproduced by
Leo Reprographics
Printed and bound by
Paramount Printing Company Ltd

First published in the United States in 1996 by Grolier Educational, Sherman Turnpike, Danbury, CT 06816

Copyright © 1996
Atlantic Europe Publishing Company Limited

Cataloging information may be obtained directly from Grolier Educational.

Set ISBN 0–7172–7572–8
Volume ISBN 0–7172–7585–X
Library of Congress Number: 95–082222

All rights reserved. No part of this publication may be reproduced, stored in a retrieval system, or transmitted in any form or by any means, electronic, mechanical, photocopying, recording or otherwise, without permission in writing of the publisher.

Acknowledgments
The publishers would like to thank the following for their kind help and advice: Steve Rockell, John Chrobnick, Tim Fulford, ICI (UK) and Rolls-Royce plc.

Picture credits
All photographs are from the **Earthscape Editions** photolibrary except the following:
(c=center t=top b=bottom l=left r=right)
courtesy of **ICI(UK)** 28b; courtesy of **Rolls-Royce plc** 23t; **USGS** 8/9t and **ZEFA** 16/17t, 40/41, 16/17

Front cover: A spectacular sample of amber-colored rhombic crystals of sulfur from Poland.
Title page: Sulfur burns in oxygen with a characteristic blue flame.

This product is manufactured from sustainable managed forests. For every tree cut down at least one more is planted.

The demonstrations described or illustrated in this book are not for replication. The Publisher cannot accept any responsibility for any accidents or injuries that may result from conducting the experiments described or illustrated in this book.

CHILDREN'S ROOM

JR546
ELEMENTS
V. 13

Contents

Introduction

An element is a substance that cannot be broken down into a simpler substance by any known means. Each of the 92 naturally occurring elements is therefore one of the fundamental materials from which everything in the Universe is made. This book is about the element sulfur.

Sulfur

Sulfur is a bright yellow, tasteless solid and a very reactive element. It is found in a wide range of minerals and is one of the products of a volcanic eruption. Perhaps this is why many people of previous centuries associated sulfur (also known as brimstone) with the unpleasant afterlife known as Hell. In the New Testament, Hell is described as a "lake that burns with fire and brimstone."

The pure element sulfur has always been thought to have strange properties. A spinning ball of it was used in one of the world's first demonstrations of static electricity. It was found that when the ball was touched by a hand, the ball began to glow.

The element sulfur is a nonmetal and will not dissolve in water. The pure element sulfur has very little smell. The smell you might associate with sulfur – bad eggs – is actually a compound of sulfur, the gas known as hydrogen sulfide. Sulfur compounds are also responsible for the smell in garlic, mustard, onions and cabbage. A sulfur compound even gives skunks their ferociously powerful and long-lasting smell.

Indeed, sulfur is a part of all living tissues. Sulfur is fixed into proteins in plants and acquired by animals who eat the plant materials.

Despite all of the unfortunate connections, sulfur has long had a beneficial medicinal role. It was used both externally, in the form of ointments for the skin and vapors, to fumigate diseased places, or internally as the medicine called brimstone. "Brimstone and treacle" was commonly used in Victorian times, and was made famous in the stories of Charles Dickens. In the modern world the group of drugs known as sulfa drugs are used as antimicrobials, one of the more important groups of medicines available today to cure infections of the digestive system.

Because sulfur occurs in all living things, it may be concentrated as tissues decay. This is why sulfur is a common (and unwelcome) component of coal, oil and, to a lesser extent, natural gas.

When these fossil fuels are burned, sulfur forms a range of gases, including sulfur dioxide, which may cause acid rain.

Sulfur dioxide is an important gas. As well as forming acid when dissolved in water, it is a bleaching agent used in many industrial processes.

The main use of sulfur in large volumes is to produce sulfuric acid, a major starting material in the production of many fertilizers.

◀ Crystals of amber-colored orthorhombic sulfur set on a rock groundmass. The other common variety, monoclinic sulfur, is shown on page 10.

Properties of sulfur

Native, or pure, sulfur is a soft, yellow, crumbly material. By heating it, many of the special properties of this element are clearly seen.

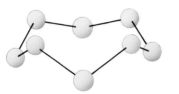

▶ The "buckled" ring structure of a molecule of one form of sulfur, as seen from the side and above.

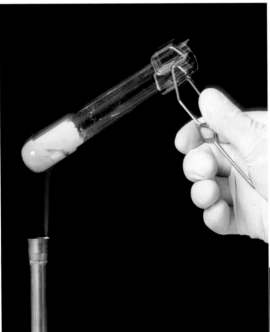

❶▶ Sulfur is usually found in a laboratory as a crumbly yellow powder. This is the starting material for the demonstrations on this page.

❷◀ Sulfur melts at 115°C. Despite this low melting temperature, it takes a long while for all of the sulfur to melt because sulfur is a poor conductor of heat.

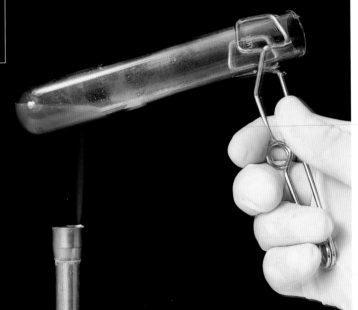

❸▶ Molten sulfur is an amber liquid that is quite runny (mobile). The reason for this is that sulfur atoms clump into "buckled" rings, each containing eight atoms. The energy of heating allows the rings to spread apart enough to slide over each other.

To imagine how this works, think of a can of spaghetti-rings. When cold, the contents of the emptied can will stand up in a saucepan (they act as a solid); but when heated, the rings start to slide around.

4▶ When more heat is applied, the sulfur darkens and the liquid becomes stickier (more viscous). When it reaches 187°C, the tube can be turned over and the liquid will not move. The extra heating has ruptured the rings, and they have formed into chains that are now entangled. (Compare the entangling to strands of spaghetti that have been stirred vigorously.)

melting point: the temperature at which a substance changes state from a solid to a liquid. It is the same as freezing point.

viscous: slow-moving, syrupy. A liquid that has a low viscosity is said to be mobile.

5▶ Heat even further (to 444°C) and the sulfur turns black. The liquid becomes mobile again because it has reached its boiling point. The extra heat energy has ruptured the chains, and they now lie in short lengths that can easily move about. (Compare this to chopping up the strands of spaghetti.)

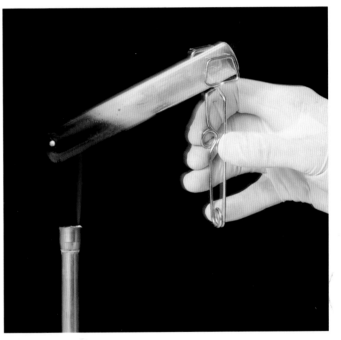

6▼ The liquid can now be poured into cold water. Pick it out of the water, and it can be stretched like rubber.

The "crash cooling" has taken energy away quickly, causing the sulfur to form enormously long chains. As it is pulled, it gets back some energy and returns to rings, gradually turning back to a solid.

▼ Part of a chain of "plastic" sulfur.

◀ "Plastic" sulfur being drawn out into "strings."

Also...

When the vapors of boiling sulfur are cooled, they condense to form "flowers of sulfur," a mixture of several kinds of sulfur.

The origin of sulfur

Sulfur is thought to have been made in the stars as enormous temperatures and pressures caused elements of lower atomic weight to fuse together.

Native sulfur is formed in many environments associated with volcanic activity, and the characteristic bright yellow sulfur crystals can be seen in many rocks surrounding volcanoes as well as in the rocks formed near geysers. Sulfur is found in most of the Earth's rocks, often as a sulfide, as well as in small amounts in all living tissue. It is also associated with salt domes.

Undersea volcanic activity

Many of the world's volcanoes erupt under the deep oceans along lines where the Earth's crustal plates split apart. At these places water seeps into the rocks and combines with the sulfur gases rising from the magma below the ocean floor. This produces eruptions of superheated acidified water that can also contain dissolved elements such as iron, zinc and copper. Flows of such water are called hydrothermal vents.

As the water flows out into the cold ocean, the cooling hydrothermal water can hold less and less sulfur in solution, and the sulfur starts to crystallize out. Over time, vents can become the sources of vast deposits of sulfur compounds called sulfides. The sulfides are compounds with other elements such as copper and iron, and as such provide potentially vital sources of metal ore.

Also...

In the deep reaches of the ocean, a wide range of living creatures depends on sulfur for life. These places have little oxygen, but a wide variety of sulfur-using bacteria have evolved that make their tissues using sulfur instead of oxygen. These form the basis of a food chain that includes worms and clams.

◄ The crater of Mt. Pinatubo. Sulfur can help predict an eruption. When a volcano is about to erupt, it produces more of the gases that will eventually burst forth, such as sulfur dioxide. Detecting an increase in sulfur dioxide emissions was one of the factors that led to the prediction of the Mt. Pinatubo eruption in the Philippines in 1991 and the eruption of Mt. Unzen in Japan.

► **Venus**
Sulfur is common on other planets in the Solar System besides Earth. For example, the main materials making up the atmosphere of the planet Venus are sulfuric acid droplets and particles of solid sulfur.

hydrothermal: a process in which hot water is involved. It is usually used in the context of rock formation because hot water and other fluids sent outward from liquid magmas are important carriers of metals and the minerals that form gemstones.

ore: a rock containing enough of a useful substance to make mining it worthwhile.

sulfide: a sulfur compound that contains no oxygen (e.g., iron sulfide – FeS).

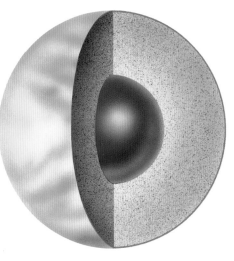

Sulfur and salt

Salt (sodium chloride) deposits are among the most common materials left behind after the evaporation of lakes in deserts. But along with the salt, other minerals are deposited, including calcium sulfate (see page 13). It is thought that sometimes the calcium sulfate was decomposed by bacteria, forming limestone and releasing native sulfur, which then formed veins within cracks in the limestone. This is a very valuable, concentrated resource, which can be melted out of the limestone using the Frasch process, described on page 17. Suitable domes of sulfur have been found in the rocks below the Gulf of Mexico, the Red Sea and Germany.

◄ Pure sulfur collects on rocks near the geysers of Rotorua, New Zealand.

Crystals of sulfur

Sulfur provides striking and colorful crystals.
All crystals form in one of seven categories, known
as the crystal systems. Some elements, such as sulfur,
can form crystals in more than one crystal system.

Sulfur produces bright yellow crystals in the
monoclinic system (in which crystals look like double-
ended chisel blades) and amber crystals in the rhombic
system (in which crystals look like three-dimensional
parallelograms, like a matchbox, the base of which has
been fixed while its top has been pushed sideways).

Brimstone is also pure sulfur, but it is not in crystalline
form. It is formed as bacteria consume hydrogen sulfide
gas in environments with no oxygen.

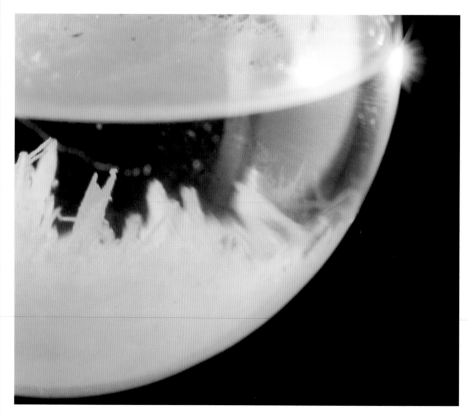

▲ To produce these beautiful monoclinic, chisellike crystals, sulfur was dissolved in hot methyl
benzene and the dissolved yellow solution allowed to cool. A hot solution can contain more
dissolved material than a cool solution, so as the solution cools, it reaches a temperature at
which the solution cannot contain any more sulfur (it is a saturated solution) and some of the
sulfur begins to form into a solid. The growing crystals act as a focus for the deposition of
more sulfur in the cooling liquid, so the crystals continue to grow.

crystal systems: there are seven patterns or systems into which all of the world's crystals can be grouped. They are: cubic, hexagonal, rhombohedral, tetragonal, orthorhombic, monoclinic and triclinic.

cubic crystal system: groupings of crystals that look like cubes.

monoclinic system: a grouping of crystals that look like double-ended chisel blades.

saturated: a state in which a liquid can hold no more of a substance. If any more of the substance is added, it will not dissolve.

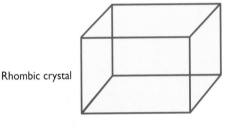

Monoclinic crystal

Rhombic crystal

▲ ◄ ◄ ▼ Sulfur crystals form in two of the crystal systems, monoclinic and rhombic. Those to the left are rhombic crystals of sulfur. Another way to identify them is by their color: rhombic crystals have an amber coloring; monoclinic crystals (such as those on the far left and below) are bright yellow.

Minerals containing sulfur

Sulfur, being a reactive element, occurs in combination with a wide range of other elements. Most of these compounds are sulfides, often known as pyrites. If the compounds also include oxygen, they are known as sulfates.

Most sulfides feel heavy because they contain heavy sulfur atoms densely packed inside the minerals. Most of the sulfides are either brassy-colored or dark, and some are very distinctive. For example, cadmium sulfide is bright orange (page 25).

Pyrite (iron sulfide) is perhaps the best known of the sulfides. Pyrite can be used as an iron ore (a rock that contains useful amounts of metal). Other main sulfur ores include galena (lead sulfide), sphalerite (zinc sulfide) and chalcopyrite (copper sulfide).

Many of the world's most important ore bodies are sulfides. The huge open pit mine at Bingham, Utah – claimed to be the world's largest man-made hole – has been dug into veins of copper sulfide. The molybdenum mine at Climax, near Leadville, Colorado, is also made from many veins of sulfide ore. When at its peak, it produced 80% of the entire world's supply of molybdenum. In Sudbury, Ontario, Canada, there are also large deposits of copper and nickel sulfides.

Sulfur is also found in calcium sulfate (as gypsum – used for Plaster of Paris and wall boards) and barium sulfate (as the very heavy mineral barite).

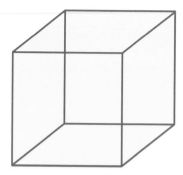

▲ Many crystals can form part of the cubic crystal system. Pyrite normally forms simple cubes, as shown above.

▲ Lead sulfide, or galena, is a common mineral found in places that have experienced volcanic activity. It is associated with zones from which miners collect other ores such as silver and tin. It is easily spotted by its dark gray cubic (box-shaped) crystals. It is also found in limestone and dolomite rocks through which heated waters have passed.

Galena is a soft mineral. When it is rubbed against a surface, it leaves a gray streak of color, showing its lead content. It is a very heavy mineral and the main source of lead for the world's industries.

Pyrite

This is the most common mineral containing sulfur. It has a brassy color that resembles gold, and for this reason it has been called "fool's gold."

Some prospectors were fooled into believing they had found a rich vein of gold when they had found a vein containing pyrite instead. It is, however, much less dense than gold and much harder. The darker form of pyrite is called marcasite.

Pyrite will react with oxygen in moist air so that the bright surface of a newly exposed pyrite quickly becomes dull and then changes to a fine gray powder.

Pyrite is found abundantly in connection with hot volcanic waters on the ocean floor, but is also formed close to places where the liquids associated with volcanic eruptions force their way into the surrounding rocks.

► Pyrite.

▼ A diagrammatic representation of the cubic structure of pyrite.

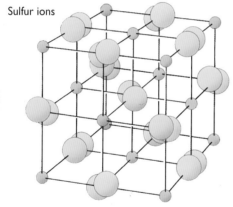

Iron ions

Sulfur ions

cubic crystal system: groupings of crystals that look like cubes.

monoclinic system: a grouping of crystals that look like double-ended chisel blades.

pyrite: "mineral of fire." This name comes from the fact that pyrite (iron sulfide) will give off sparks if struck with a stone.

sulfate: a compound that includes sulfur and oxygen, for example, calcium sulfate or gypsum.

▼ Copper sulfide ore.

◄ These are desert roses, made from calcium sulfate or gypsum. The crystals of this mineral look a bit like rose petals, hence its name. The monoclinic crystals give it a different look than the more blocklike cubic crystals of pyrite.

Reactivity of sulfur

Sulfur is one of the most reactive of all the elements. This is why sulfur will react with most metals (in the absence of air) to form sulfides and why many sulfur compounds are sulfides.

Sulfur will also react with oxygen in the air (a piece of iron sulfide left lying around will eventually change to iron sulfate) and will readily burn in oxygen to produce sulfur dioxide gas.

In this demonstration, some sulfur powder is placed on a suitable metal holder and ignited in air. It is then introduced into a gas jar filled with oxygen, where it burns with a blue flame.

❶▶ Some powdered sulfur, oxygen in a gas jar and a deflagrating spoon (a metal spoon in which sulfur is burned). Notice that the deflagrating spoon has a metal disc above it in order to protect anyone holding the spoon while the sulfur is burning. The disc also serves as a support for holding the spoon on the middle of the gas jar (as to the right).

Also...
Deflagration is the old word for combustion, hence "deflagrating spoon."

EQUATION: Burning sulfur in air
Sulfur + oxygen ⇨ sulfur dioxide
$S(s)$ + $O_2(g)$ ⇨ $SO_2(g)$

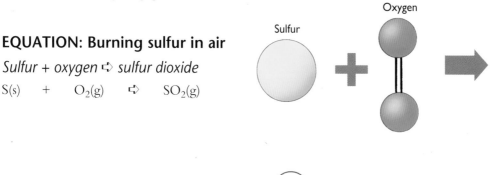

Sulfur   Oxygen

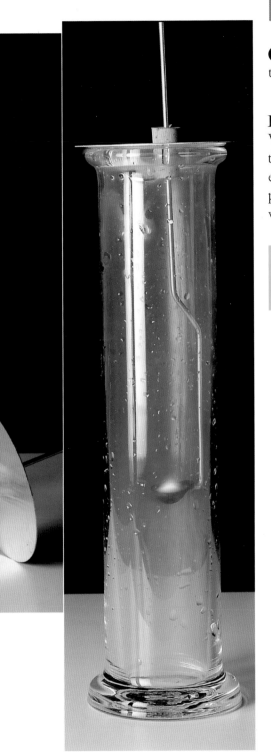

combustion: the special case of oxidization of a substance in which a considerable amount of heat and usually light are given out. Combustion is often referred to as "burning."

❷◄ The sulfur is ignited in air and then introduced to the oxygen, where it burns with a bright blue flame.

Burning sulfur compounds

When sulfur or sulfur-containing compounds are burned, the reaction always produces sulfur dioxide gas, as the example equation below shows. This can be a major problem for the iron- and copper-refining industries as well as for power stations burning sulfur-rich coal or oil.

EQUATION: Burning sulfide ore

Iron sulfide + oxygen ⇨ iron oxide + sulfur dioxide

$$4FeS(s) \ + \ 7O_2(g) \ ⇨ \ 2Fe_2O_3(s) \ + \ 4SO_2(g)$$

Cubic crystals of pyrite

▲▶ Pyrite (iron sulfide) often occurs in brassy-colored cubic crystals (see page 13). However, all sulfides form in the absence of air. Sulfur reacts so readily with oxygen that when it is exposed to the air, especially damp air, the crystals quickly oxidize to iron sulfate. The glass jar on the right, for example, once contained perfect cubic crystals, but these have now oxidized to gray iron sulfate and therefore fallen apart. For this reason, if you want to keep samples of pyrite that you might have collected, they should be protected from contact with damp air.

EQUATION: Weathering of pyrite (iron sulfide) in damp air

Iron sulfide + water + oxygen ⇨ iron sulfate + sulfuric acid

$$2FeS_2(s) \ + \ 2H_2O(l) \ + \ 7O_2(g) \ ⇨ \ 2FeSO_4(s) \ + \ 2H_2SO_4(aq)$$

Extracting sulfur

For centuries it was commonplace to collect sulfur by lowering people down the inside of volcanoes in baskets so they could scrape the sulfur off the walls of the vents. Needless to say, this was not a very popular occupation.

The main technique used to recover sulfur from buried deposits of native sulfur, such as those associated with salt domes (see pages 8 and 9), relies on the fact that sulfur has a low melting point, while at the same time being insoluble in water.

Superheated water (raised to a temperature of about 165°C) is pumped underground through a pipe. Inside this pipe are two smaller pipes. Compressed air is pumped down the central pipe, and a frothy mixture of liquid sulfur, water and air is pushed up through the remaining pipe. This system is called the Frasch process, named for its inventor Herman Frasch, an American chemist who devised the process in 1891.

Most sulfur mined by the Frasch process is transported as liquid in insulated railway cars and ships and taken to sulfuric acid plants.

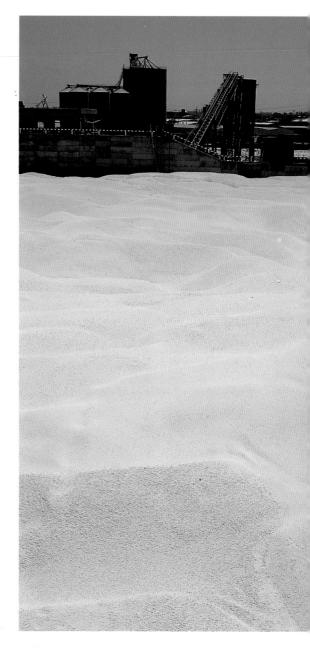

Sulfur from pyrites

In the past, many sulfide-rich ores have been roasted, not to recover the metals but to produce compounds of sulfur. The roasting of pyrite produces sulfur dioxide gas, which can then be converted to sulfuric acid (see page 26).

Sulfur from fossil fuels

Although natural gas has a lower sulfur content than the other fossil fuels, it is still important to recover that sulfur and prevent pollution.

The sulfur is obtained by reacting hydrogen sulfide contained in the natural gas with oxygen. This produces sulfur dioxide gas, which can then be made into sulfuric acid by reacting the sulfur dioxide with oxygen and water.

Sulfur as a byproduct

All fossil fuels, as well as many metal ores, produce large volumes of sulfur-containing gas when they are heated. For a long time natural gas has been the main source of non-Frasch sulfur, because the sulfur had to be removed before the gas could be sold. Other producers of sulfur gases simply released them to the air.

With the tightening of regulations for the emission of sulfur, much of the sulfur required for modern industry is now recovered from fossil fuels by "scrubbing" the smokestack gases as they rise up from power stations and metal refineries that burn copper and lead sulfide ores.

Not only does this collect sulfur efficiently, but it reduces the amount of acid rain in the atmosphere. The extra production of sulfur from these sources has coincided with an increase in demand for sulfur for making fertilizers.

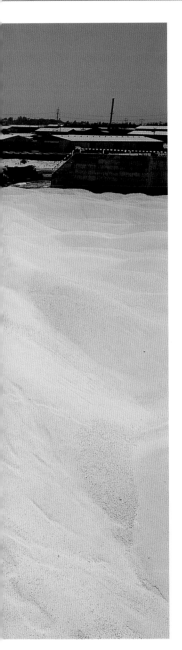

▲ Sulfur is dried and stored before use.

▶ The Frasch process of sulfur extraction involves pumping superheated water (water under pressure and heated to above 100°C) into a sulfur-bearing deposit. The sulfur does not react with water, so when it is pumped up to the surface, the result is a suspension of sulfur in water. Another word for suspension is a mixture.

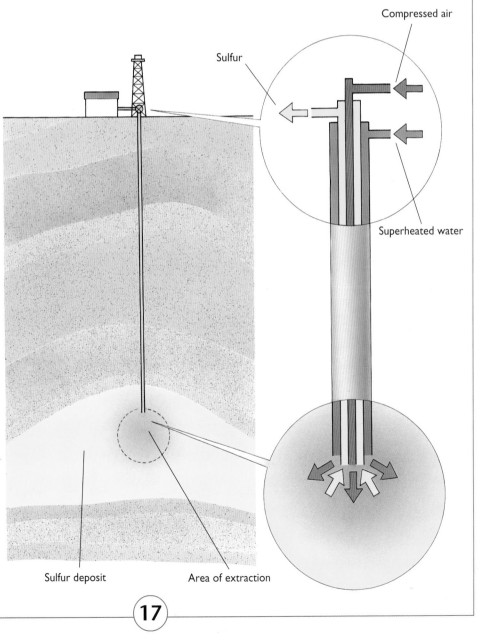

Compressed air

Sulfur

Superheated water

Sulfur deposit   Area of extraction

Sulfur dioxide

Sulfur dioxide is one of the most important sulfur gases. It is a dense, colorless gas with a choking (pungent) smell.

In large concentrations sulfur dioxide can cause suffocation, while even small amounts can combine with water droplets to make acid rain. For these reasons, sulfur dioxide is regarded as a health hazard. In addition it is partly responsible for harming vegetation and corroding limestone buildings.

Sulfur dioxide is a pollutant but also has many valuable uses. For example, it is a very good bleaching agent, and many factories producing paper and textiles rely on it. Sulfur dioxide is also used in food warehouses because it is helpful in preserving both fruit and vegetables.

Preparing sulfur dioxide in the laboratory

Sulfur dioxide can be prepared by burning sulfur in oxygen as shown on pages 14 and 15, but more usually it is made by adding dilute sulfuric acid to a salt of sulfurous acid called a sulfite. Sulfites are generally used as bleaching agents.

EQUATION: Preparation of sulfur dioxide gas from a sulfur salt

Sulfuric acid + sodium sulfite ⇨ sulfur dioxide + sodium sulfate + water

$$H_2SO_4(aq) \quad + \quad Na_2SO_3(s) \quad ⇨ \quad SO_2(g) \quad + \quad Na_2SO_4(aq) \quad + \quad H_2O(l)$$

Properties of sulfur dioxide gas

Sulfur dioxide is an acidic gas, that is, when dissolved in water, a weak acid is produced, called sulfurous acid.

Sulfur dioxide is a reducing agent and will take oxygen from other substances. As a result, it can act as a bleach (see page 20).

Making use of sulfur dioxide

Sulfur dioxide can be used to produce sulfuric acid, a chemical used in fertilizer production. Some of the sulfur dioxide created by power stations is now recovered from the smokestacks rather than released into the environment (see page 22).

Sulfur dioxide can also be used as a bleaching agent because of its reducing properties. It is used to bleach wood pulp in making paper.

◄ Acid rain is responsible for damage to trees on already acid soils.

acid: compounds containing hydrogen that can attack and dissolve many substances. Acids are described as weak or strong, dilute or concentrated, mineral or organic.

strong acid: an acid that has completely dissociated (ionized) in water. Mineral acids are strong acids.

weak acid: an acid that has only partly dissociated (ionized) in water. Most organic acids are weak acids.

EQUATIONS: The reactions in the creation of acid rain
Stage 1: Sulfur dioxide gas emissions created by burning sulfur-containing impurities in petroleum

Hydrogen sulfide + oxygen ⇨ water + sulfur dioxide

$$2H_2S(g) + 3O_2(g) \Rightarrow 2H_2O(l) + 2SO_2(g)$$

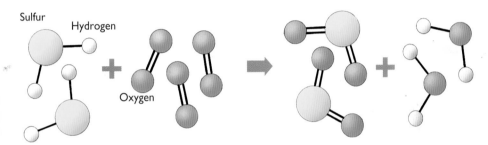

Sulfur

Hydrogen

Oxygen

How sulfur dioxide in air makes acid rain

When sulfur dioxide dissolves in water, the result is sulfurous acid. This is part of the environmental problem called acid rain (see page 22). But sulfur dioxide is also oxidized by oxygen in the air to make sulfur trioxide. When sulfur trioxide dissolves in raindrops, it produces the strong acid sulfuric acid, which has a far more severe impact on the environment than the weak sulfurous acid.

Stage 2: Creating sulfur trioxide

Sulfur dioxide + oxygen ⇨ sulfur trioxide

$$2SO_2(g) + O_2(g) \Rightarrow 2SO_3(g)$$

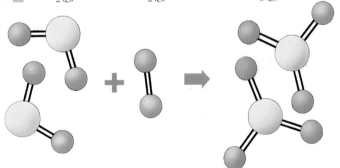

Stage 3: Dissolving sulfur trioxide in raindrops

Sulfur trioxide + water ⇨ sulfuric acid

$$SO_3(g) + H_2O(l) \Rightarrow H_2SO_4(aq)$$

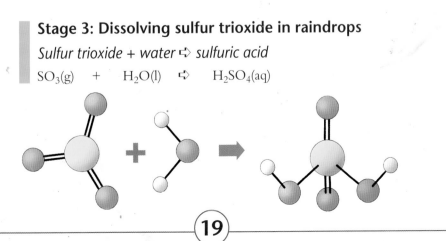

Sulfur dioxide as a bleaching agent

Any chemical that makes a material brighter and makes stains invisible is called a bleach. Bleaches also kill bacteria.

A bleach removes stains by reacting with the stain, making it colorless. Bleaches work either by adding oxygen to or removing it from the stained material. The colorless product is often more soluble and so is also more easily removed by detergents.

A number of sulfur-based products are used on a large scale for industrial bleaching. Sodium peroxydisulfate is used as a domestic bleach for home laundry applications because it is safer than chlorine-based bleaches on delicate textiles. It is an example of a bleach that oxidizes the staining material.

Sodium sulfite and sulfur dioxide are used as industrial bleaches, especially for wood pulp. They act in the opposite way, reducing materials by removing oxygen from them.

Bread bleach

Sulfur dioxide is not a strong bleach and so can be used to bleach silk, wool and even flour (white flour for white bread). Sulfur dioxide will work on most dyes containing oxygen. In this case the sulfur dioxide acts as a reducing agent taking oxygen from the dye and making it colorless. But note that this process is reversible. The dye gradually picks up oxygen from the air and becomes colored again. This is why, for example, straw hats that were white when new gradually turn yellow (the original color of the straw containing natural dyes).

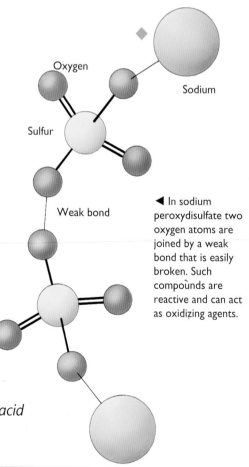

Oxygen

Sodium

Sulfur

Weak bond

◄ In sodium peroxydisulfate two oxygen atoms are joined by a weak bond that is easily broken. Such compounds are reactive and can act as oxidizing agents.

▲ White bread is made with flour that has been bleached using sulfur dioxide. Some brown bread also uses bleached white flour that has subsequently been dyed.

Colored dye + <u>sulfurous</u> acid (sulfur dioxide + water) react to yield colorless dye + <u>sulfuric</u> acid

oxidizing agent: a substance that removes electrons from another substance (and therefore is itself reduced).

reducing agent: a substance that gives electrons to another substance. Sulfur dioxide is a reducing agent used for bleaching bread.

▲▶ These pansies show the effect of sulfur dioxide bleaching. A purple pansy was exposed to a sulfur dioxide atmosphere for two minutes and then put back in water, where it turned yellow. If it had been subjected to an even longer exposure, it would have turned completely white (colorless).

Sulfur dioxide and the environment

The oxides of sulfur (sulfur dioxide, sulfur trioxide) are often referred to as "SO_x" for short. Sulfur dioxide is produced naturally when volcanoes erupt and when forests catch fire or vegetation decays.

But in our industrial world about as much sulfur dioxide is produced by industry (some 150 million tons a year) as from natural processes. This means that instead of a natural amount of 10 parts per billion of sulfur dioxide in the air, the modern world experiences 20 parts per billion. In cities, on calm, foggy days, this level can rise to over 100 parts per billion, well within the zone of danger to health.

Polluting sulfur dioxide is produced when sulfurous fossil fuels are burned, so the main contributors are coal and oil-fired power stations and home heating systems. Natural gas is increasingly being used as a power station fuel because it contains relatively little sulfur. The fraction of petroleum used for making gasoline also has little sulfur, which means that vehicles are not major producers of sulfur-based gases.

Smoke and sulfur dioxide

Smoke is a mixture of both small solids and gases, one of the most important of which is sulfur dioxide. When sulfur dioxide is breathed in, the gas combines with the water in the mouth and throat, adding to the acidity of these areas and often causing irritation. In higher concentrations it can cause sore throats.

However, when smoky fumes are breathed in, some of the sulfur dioxide is condensed on the tiny smoke particles, and in this form it can be breathed right down into the lungs before it combines with water and turns into an acid. Here it can cause breathing problems and (like smoking) can also be a cause of lung cancer.

The world's most famous smoky fog, in which smoke particles and sulfur dioxide were present in high concentrations, was the Great London Smog (smoky fog) of 1952, when nearly 4,000 people died in five days as a result of the suffocating air. This famous episode led to new laws in most industrial countries designed to keep levels of sulfur dioxide in the air under control. For example, smoky coals can no longer be burned in most city hearths or used to fuel boilers. Instead "smokeless" fuels must be used.

Also...

One of the most important catalysts in the air is an exhaust gas of vehicles, nitrogen dioxide. Sulfur dioxide will not naturally react with oxygen in the air, but nitrogen dioxide combines readily with sulfur dioxide to make the sulfur trioxide that will combine with raindrops to make sulfuric acid, which then falls as acid rain.

During the reaction the nitrogen dioxide gives up some oxygen, but it can immediately get this back from the surrounding air, so in the end, no nitrogen dioxide is used up at all.

▶ A power station using brown coal (lignite). The clouds coming from the cooling towers are harmless water vapor. The polluting materials come from the tall chimneys (smokestacks). Traditionally, such chimneys were built tall to disperse the sulfur dioxide coming from them. Now most such power stations have "scrubbers" built into the chimney system to remove the sulfur dioxide. As a result, what is emitted from chimneys is now mostly particles of soot and carbon dioxide gas.

acidity: a general term for the strength of an acid in a solution.

smoke: a mixture of both small solids and gases.

Electrostatic precipitators

Many new power stations are being built with electrostatic precipitators built into the chimney system. An electrostatic precipitator uses static electrical charges to cause sulfur particles to be precipitated from the flue gases. This leaves the exhaust cleaner and less liable to cause acid rain. The sulfur collected can be used for other purposes (see pages 18 and 19), thus providing a way of offsetting the cost of the equipment.

◀ These are electrostatic precipitators fitted to a new 1000 MW power station in India to remove the sulfur from the exhaust gases. The electrostatic precipitators are in the foreground of the picture.

EQUATION: Removing sulfur dioxide from power station exhausts with sodium hydroxide

Sulfur dioxide + sodium hydroxide ⇨ sodium sulfate + water

$$SO_2(g) \quad + \quad 2NaOH(aq) \quad ⇨ \quad Na_2SO_3(s) \quad + \quad H_2O(l)$$

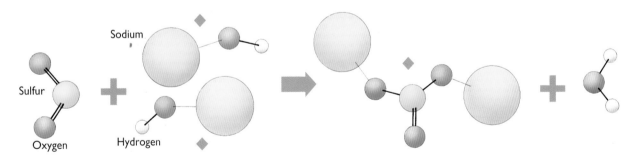

Sulfur

Oxygen

Sodium

Hydrogen

Pollution that crosses borders

Sulfur dioxide is a gas, so it can be carried large distances from where it is produced. This means that, for example, sulfur dioxide released by power stations in one place can carry for thousands of kilometers downwind, where it might combine with water droplets in a cloud and cause acid rain that harms trees.

In the most extreme cases, pollution caused in one country can cause acid rain damage in another country. This is most likely to be the case in both Europe and North America. In Europe the coals used in power stations in eastern Europe have produced pollution that has killed trees in the Black Forest of Germany; pollution produced in Britain may have harmed forests in Norway and Sweden and pollution caused in the northeastern United States and southeastern Canada has harmed forests in eastern North America.

Hydrogen sulfide

Hydrogen sulfide gas burns with a blue flame. It is a reducing agent, taking oxygen from some of the compounds with which it reacts.

It is poorly soluble in water, but when dissolved will produce a solution of hydrogen sulfide with a smell of bad eggs.

When hydrogen sulfide reacts with other compounds to produce new sulfide compounds, they are characteristically black in color (the exceptions are pyrite, which is yellow, and cadmium sulfide, which is orange.) Precipitating black lead sulfide from a solution of a lead salt by passing hydrogen sulfide over it is used as a laboratory test for hydrogen sulfide.

▲ Lead nitrate and hydrogen sulfide produce a black precipitate of lead sulfide (the mineral form of this is galena).

▼ Cobalt sulfide

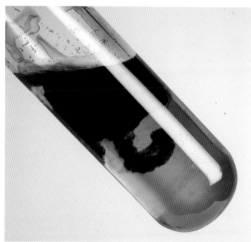

Preparing hydrogen sulfide in the laboratory
Hydrogen sulfide is normally prepared by adding dilute hydrochloric acid to iron sulfide.

EQUATION: Preparing hydrogen sulfide

Dilute hydrochloric acid + iron sulfide ⇨ ferric chloride + hydrogen sulfide

$$2HCl(aq) \quad + \quad FeS(s) \quad ⇨ \quad FeCl_2(aq) \quad + \quad H_2S(g)$$

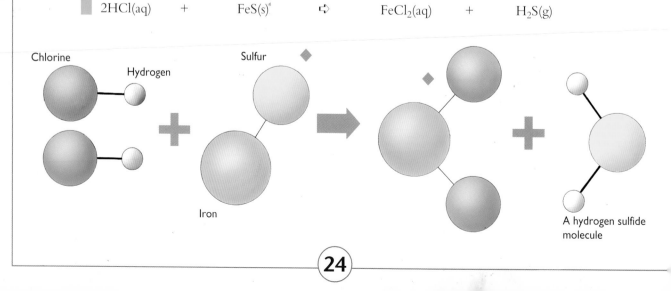

Chlorine
Hydrogen
Sulfur
Iron
A hydrogen sulfide molecule

▲ Nickel sulfide

▼ Cadmium sulfide

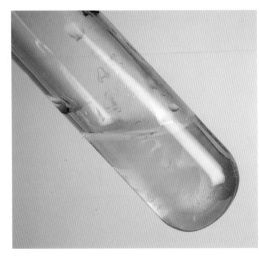

pyrite: "mineral of fire." This name comes from the fact that pyrite (iron sulfide) will give off sparks if struck with a stone.

reducing agent: a substance that gives electrons to another substance. Sulfur dioxide is a reducing agent used for bleaching bread.

Hydrogen sulfide smells like rotten eggs

Hydrogen sulfide is present in natural gas and is also produced during the decay of dead material in the absence of water. This is one reason that some decaying remains and stagnant waters have a bad smell.

Hydrogen sulfide smells like rotten eggs. The odor occurs when the proteins of dead tissue that contain sulfur begin to decompose.

Tarnishing

Hydrogen sulfide is the polluting gas that reacts with silver in the atmosphere to produce black tarnishing (silver sulfide) on silverware.

Poisonous hydrogen sulfide

Hydrogen sulfide is a highly poisonous gas, which, because it has no color, can only be detected by its smell. In fact, all the gases of sulfur (SO_X) are poisonous, and most have unpleasant, choking odors.

Because SO_X gases quickly paralyze the nerves in the nose, their smell soon *appears* to go away. This is very dangerous effect because it encourages people to remain in contact with the gas rather than move away.

Also...

Many fossil fuels contain sulfides, which are soluble in water. As water seeps into mine workings, it dissolves the sulfides and may subsequently find its way into groundwater or streams, where it can cause widespread and serious pollution. This is why the water pumped from active mines has to be carefully treated before being discharged.

EQUATION: Removing sulfur-containing impurities such as hydrogen sulfide from petroleum with sodium hydroxide

Hydrogen sulfide + sodium hydroxide ⇨ sodium sulfide + water

$$H_2S(g) + 2NaOH(aq) \Rightarrow Na_2S(s) + 2H_2O(l)$$

Sulfuric acid

Sulfuric acid, a colorless, thick, heavy and "oily" liquid, is one of the most common acids used in industry and the laboratory. It is a strong mineral acid.

Dilute sulfuric acid will react with most metals to form sulfate compounds and release hydrogen gas. It reacts with bases to form sulfates and water only.

Concentrated sulfuric acid is also a dehydrating agent, so that it will remove water from other compounds. For example, if a piece of sugar is placed in sulfuric acid, it becomes a black lump of carbon, as all the water is removed from the sugar molecules.

If sulfuric acid touches human skin, the molecules in the skin immediately begin to lose water. This is an acid burn.

▲ Sulfuric acid reacts with metals such as zinc to produce a sulfate of the metal and release hydrogen gas.

Also...

When water and a concentrated acid mix, a huge amount of heat is given off. Water should never be added to concentrated acid. Rather, the acid should be stirred slowly into the water. If water is added to the acid, the water boils as it enters the acid, causing it to splash out much like hot fat in a fryer. The result could be dangerous acid burns.

EQUATION: Reaction of dilute sulfuric acid and zinc metal

Sulfuric acid + zinc ⇨ zinc sulfate + hydrogen

$$H_2SO_4(aq) + Zn(s) \Rightarrow ZnSO_4(aq) + H_2(g)$$

A dehydrating agent

The demonstration on these two pages shows how water can be removed from sugar by dehydration using sulfuric acid.

❶▶ A layer of sugar is placed in a beaker, and concentrated sulfuric acid is added.

EQUATION: Dehydration of sucrose using concentrated sulfuric acid

Sucrose + sulfuric acid ⇨ steam + carbon + sulfuric acid

$$C_{12}H_{22}O_{11}(s) + H_2SO_4(l) \Rightarrow 11H_2O(g) + 12C(s) + H_2SO$$

corrosive: a substance, either an acid or an alkali, that *rapidly* attacks a wide range of other substances.

mineral acid: an acid that does not contain carbon and which attacks minerals. Hydrochloric, sulfuric and nitric acids are the main mineral acids.

strong acid: an acid that has completely dissociated (ionized) in water. Mineral acids are strong acids.

❷▲❸▼ The sugar will turn yellow, brown and finally black.

❹▲ Suddenly the surface will bulge up and crack. By now so much heat is given out that much of the surplus water produced by the reaction will form steam, but the steam bubbles are trapped in the sticky carbon and they simply expand in the "goo," making it frothy. When it sets, it is like a piece of coke.

Manufacturing sulfuric acid

More sulfuric acid is made than almost any other substance. This is because the acid is useful in making so many other products.

Sulfuric acid is made by reacting sulfur dioxide with oxygen and water. Sulfur dioxide is obtained either from hydrogen sulfide in natural gas or as pure sulfur is burned in air. It may also be collected from power station smokestacks.

Sulfur dioxide reacts only slowly with oxygen, so the process is made quicker by reacting the substances at a high temperature (500°C) and in the presence of a catalyst. The catalyst used in this reaction (called the Contact process) is a material called vanadium pentoxide.

Sulfur dioxide and air are forced through a tower containing the catalyst in the form of pellets. The sulfur trioxide gas then flows into a tower containing quartz bathed in a circulating bath of sulfuric acid. As the gas dissolves in the sulfuric acid, the acid becomes more concentrated, and some is drawn off and diluted.

The gas is not added directly to water because this would give off too much heat energy and make the water evaporate.

The Contact process

Sulfur dioxide and oxygen are brought together in a converter containing vanadium pentoxide. Usually more than one stage of conversion is needed. The reaction produces heat. If the reacting gases get too hot, they stop reacting, so the gases are led from one converter, cooled and then fed into another. Up to four stages of this conversion are needed. By this time nearly all of the sulfur dioxide has been converted to sulfur trioxide.

The absorber is a tank of sulfuric acid that absorbs sulfur trioxide, concentrating the sulfuric acid even further. Some of this liquid can be drawn off and diluted as required. Sulfur trioxide is not added to water because it releases a great deal of heat and produces a fine mist that is difficult to handle.

◀ A bank of Contact process converters.

The Contact process.

Sulfur dioxide (SO_2) and oxygen (O_2)

① Converter containing vanadium pentoxide catalyst achieves 63% conversion to sulfur trioxide.

Gases cooled

② Converter containing vanadium pentoxide catalyst achieves 84% conversion to sulfur trioxide.

Gases cooled

③ Converter containing vanadium pentoxide catalyst achieves 93% conversion to sulfur trioxide.

SO_3 fed to an absorber

Sulfur trioxide absorbed to create 99.5% sulfuric acid, which is then diluted to 98% acid.

Remaining SO_3

④ Converter containing vanadium pentoxide catalyst achieves 99.5% conversion to sulfur trioxide.

Gases fed to an absorber

Remaining sulfur trioxide absorbed to create 99.5% sulfuric acid, which is then diluted to 98% acid.

catalyst: a substance that speeds up a chemical reaction but itself remains unaltered at the end of the reaction.

EQUATION: Stage 1: Reacting sulfur dioxide and oxygen to produce sulfur trioxide

Sulfur dioxide gas + oxygen ⇨ sulfur trioxide

$$2SO_2(g) \quad + \quad O_2(g) \quad ⇨ \quad 2SO_3(g)$$

Sulfur

Oxygen

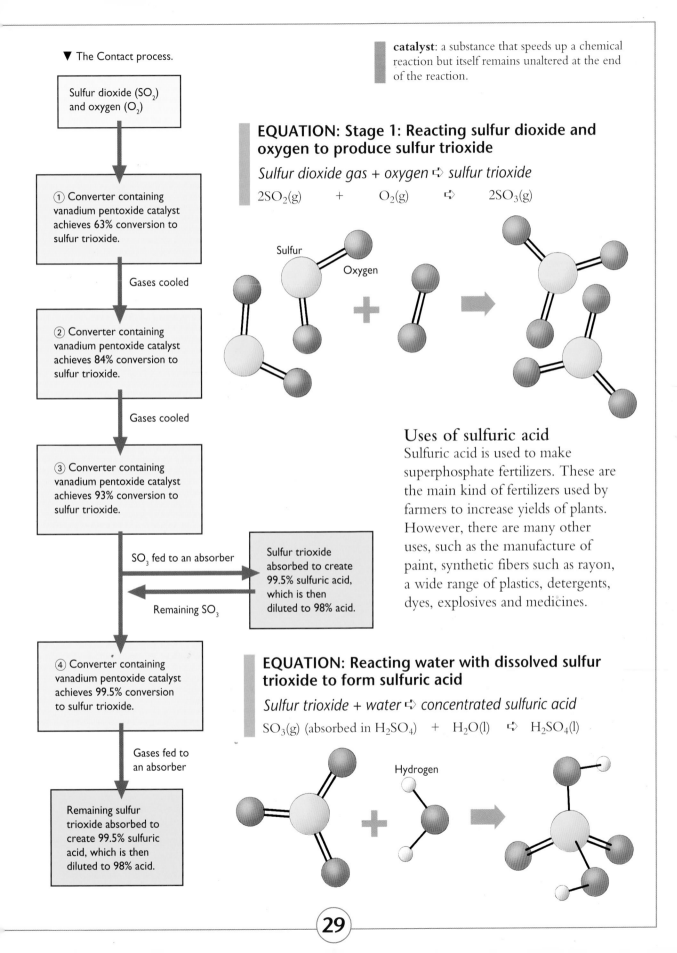

Uses of sulfuric acid

Sulfuric acid is used to make superphosphate fertilizers. These are the main kind of fertilizers used by farmers to increase yields of plants. However, there are many other uses, such as the manufacture of paint, synthetic fibers such as rayon, a wide range of plastics, detergents, dyes, explosives and medicines.

EQUATION: Reacting water with dissolved sulfur trioxide to form sulfuric acid

Sulfur trioxide + water ⇨ concentrated sulfuric acid

$$SO_3(g) \text{ (absorbed in } H_2SO_4) \quad + \quad H_2O(l) \quad ⇨ \quad H_2SO_4(l)$$

Hydrogen

Sulfuric acid as an electrolyte

Dilute sulfuric acid is used in vehicle batteries, sometimes called "wet batteries," and more accurately called "secondary batteries." They are called secondary batteries because the cells inside the battery can be recharged. (Contrast this with a primary cell, like a dry cell, in which the chemicals inside the cell react to produce electricity only once.) In a vehicle battery six cells are combined to give the 12 volt supply that vehicles use worldwide.

Lead-acid batteries are the most commonly used form of vehicle battery. To work as an electrical battery, each of the cells inside it must have two electrodes made of electrically conducting materials. These must be bathed in a liquid that can conduct electricity as well as help the battery store electricity. This material is called an electrolyte.

▶ Lead-acid batteries are designed to give each electrode a large surface area. This allows it to change stored chemical energy into electrical energy quickly. The electrodes are made from a lead alloy; half are covered in a paste of lead sulfate. All the electrodes are bathed in dilute sulfuric acid.

Negative electrode made of lead

Positive electrode made of lead dioxide

Sulfuric acid electrolyte

Operation of the battery

As the battery is charged (perhaps from a vehicle generator), and a current is passed through the battery, a chemical reaction occurs that increases the concentration of the sulfuric acid and forms a coating of lead and lead dioxide on the electrodes. This process is electrolysis (the same process that puts chromium coatings on cutlery, gold and silver-plating on ornaments and tin-plate on steel food cans).

When the battery is called upon to discharge electricity, the reaction reverses, the lead coatings are converted to lead sulfate and the sulfuric acid is used up.

This process can be repeated many times, giving the secondary cell a useful life of many years of constant service.

▼ A secondary battery works by converting chemical energy to electrical energy. For this to happen there have to be two different materials as electrodes and an electron-carrying liquid, an electrolyte. The condition of the electrolyte changes as it charges and discharges.

acidity: a general term for the strength of an acid in a solution.

electrode: a conductor that forms one terminal of a cell.

electrolyte: a solution that conducts electricity.

ion: an atom, or group of atoms, that has gained or lost one or more electrons and so developed an electrical charge. Ions carry electrical current through solutions.

Sulfuric acid electrolyte

Negative electrode made of lead

Positive electrode made of lead dioxide

❶▶ The battery is fully charged. The negative electrode is formed of spongy lead, and the positive electrode is lead dioxide. The concentration of sulfuric acid is at a maximum.

❷▼ The battery is being discharged through use. The two electrode materials begin to be converted to lead sulfate. The concentration of sulfuric acid is decreasing.

Lead sulfate is deposited on both electrodes.

❸◀ The battery is fully discharged. The electrodes are now covered with lead sulfate and the sulfuric acid concentration is very low. (Charging the battery using a generator will return the battery to the state in ❶.)

Measuring the charge of a battery by its sulfuric acid concentration

As the cell gives out its electricity, the sulfuric acid is used up and becomes more dilute. This means that the state of charge of a battery can be measured by its acid concentration using a hydrometer.

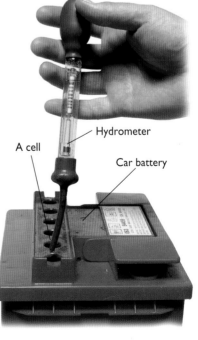

Hydrometer

A cell

Car battery

▶ A hydrometer. The acid is drawn up the syringe by squeezing and then releasing the rubber bulb. The float inside the hydrometer is marked with colored bands. The higher the float rises, the more concentrated the acid, the greater the acid density, the better the battery charge. Floats that sink low in the hydrometer show a weak (low density) electrolyte and thus a dilute acid. This means that the battery is discharged.

Sulfates and sulfites

Sulfates are compounds containing sulfur and oxygen. Sulfites are compounds of sulfur containing less oxygen than sulfates.

There is a wide range of sulfates, usually formed by a combination of a metal, such as calcium, magnesium or sodium, as shown on this page, or copper, as shown on page 34.

Sulfate salts are formed in the laboratory by reacting sulfuric acid on a metal, oxide, hydroxide or carbonate.

Most sulfates are soluble in water.

▲ Gypsum is used for plastering in the construction industry.

Magnesium sulfate

Magnesium sulfate was first made by evaporating mineral water from a spring near a town called Epsom in Surrey, England. For this reason it is also called Epsom salts.

Epsom salts act as a laxative by preventing the water in the intestine from being absorbed in the body. The result is that there is more water than usual in the intestine, which sets the action of the bowels in motion.

Concentrated Epsom salts are used to stop inflammation and to prevent convulsions. They are also used in both dyeing and bleaching processes, as part of fertilizers, in matches and explosives. They can also have a fireproofing effect.

Calcium sulfate

One of the most common sulfate minerals in the Earth's rocks is calcium sulfate, also known as gypsum. One form of gypsum is alabaster which, being soft, is easily machined to make ornaments such as candlesticks.

Gypsum is formed in the bottom of saline lakes. As the lake water evaporates, the chemicals dissolved in it become progressively more concentrated until the solution becomes saturated and crystals begin to form.

Crushed gypsum is used as Plaster of Paris and is made into wallboard (it is the smooth surface of the interiors of walls).

▼ Sulfates and their properties

Sulfate	Common name	Application
Calcium sulfate	Gypsum Plaster of Paris	Soil conditioner, plasterboard Casts (used to set broken limbs)
Barium sulfate	Barite	Drilling mud in oil fields, digestion, X-rays
Sodium sulfate	Glauber's salt	Glass-making
Lead sulfate		Produced as lead-acid battery discharges
Copper sulfate	Blue vitriol	Fungicide (Bordeaux mixture)
Iron sulfate	Green vitriol	Lawn care
Magnesium sulfate	Epsom salts	Laxative

Sodium sulfate

Also known as Glauber's salt, sodium sulfate is commonly found dissolved in drinking water. Sodium sulfate occurs as thick evaporite beds and can be mined by pumping hot water down a well and pumping the dissolved sulfate back up.

Sodium sulfate is used instead of sulfuric acid for some processes, for example, in making dyes, paper and glass, and to help molten metals flow (when used as a flux).

Sodium sulfate crystals melt at 32°C, meaning that they will melt at high room temperatures. On melting they absorb very large amounts of heat (the salt has a large latent heat). This means that sodium sulfate can be used in some forms of solar storage heating. The Sun's rays can be used to melt the sulfate; and later, as it cools and solidifies during the night, it releases its heat.

▲ Sodium thiosulfate crystals

flux: a material used to make it easier for a liquid to flow. A flux dissolves metal oxides and so prevents a metal from oxidizing while being heated.

latent heat: the amount of heat that is absorbed or released during the process of changing state between gas, liquid or solid. For example, heat is absorbed when a substance melts and it is released again when the substance solidifies.

saturated solution: a solution that holds the maximum possible amount of dissolved material. The amount of material in solution varies with the temperature; cold solutions can hold less dissolved solid material than hot solutions. Gases are more soluble in cold liquids than hot liquids.

Also...Photographer's hypo

Every time you have a photograph printed, the printer will have used a chemical called hypo. This is short for the chemical sodium thiosulfate. It is used to "fix" the image after it has been developed.

The photographic film contains a surface coating, or emulsion, of chemicals. This emulsion, a kind of gelatin, contains minute crystals or grains of silver compounds spread evenly over it The smaller the size of the crystals, the finer the grain and the better the eventual picture quality. (This is why we talk about "graininess" when referring to photograph quality.)

When the camera shutter is worked, the iris opens on the camera and light reaches the emulsion of the film. The light causes a chemical reaction to occur that results in small groups of silver atoms clumping together. Wherever silver atoms clump together within a crystal or grain, they will provide the image on the film.

Developing a negative requires several chemical stages. The first chemical stage happens in a darkroom, where the developer solution converts the clumps of silver atoms into tiny particles of pure silver.

However, the emulsion still contains a mix of chemicals that would react to light and fog the film; this mix has to be removed before the film can be exposed to the light. This is the job of the hypo. The hypo dissolves away the remaining silver-containing compounds. After fixing, the film is stable, and all other processing can be done in normal light.

The hypo reacts with the silver compounds of the emulsion that have not been changed to pure silver but leaves the pure silver alone. When the film is washed in water, everything except the silver is removed, and the film surface contains just silver. The film is now a "negative" in which all light areas are shown dark and all dark areas are shown transparent or light. The positive print (the actual photograph) is produced by shining a light through the negative onto a piece of light-sensitive printing paper.

EQUATION: Making photographer's hypo

Sodium sulfite + sulfur ⇨ sodium thiosulfate

$$Na_2SO_3(aq) \quad + \quad S(s) \quad ⇨ \quad Na_2S_2O_3(aq)$$

Copper sulfate

Copper sulfate occurs as a blue solution or crystals. It can be made by reacting sulfuric acid and copper carbonate.

Copper sulfate is widely used as a fungicide. Originally it was probably used in a pure form as a seed covering to protect the seed from rotting before it could germinate. Later it was combined with lime to make Bordeaux mixture (see page 42). It is also used to treat wood and preserve it from attack by fungi, molds and other rotting organisms.

A white form of copper sulfate (called anhydrous copper sulfate) will absorb large amounts of water and can therefore be used as a drying agent. Anhydrous copper sulfate can also be used as a simple test for the presence of water because it changes from white to blue.

Preparing copper sulfate
Dilute sulfuric acid and green copper carbonate produce a blue solution of copper sulfate.

▲▶ Sulfuric acid is added to copper carbonate powder to produce a solution of copper sulfate that can be evaporated, leaving copper sulfate crystals. A copper sulfate solution can also be produced by adding sulfuric acid to black copper oxide powder.

EQUATION: Reaction of sulfuric acid and copper carbonate

Sulfuric acid + copper carbonate ⇨ copper sulfate + carbon dioxide + water

$$H_2SO_4(aq) \quad + \quad CuCO_3(s) \quad ⇨ \quad CuSO_4(aq) \quad + \quad CO_2(g) \quad + \quad H_2O(l)$$

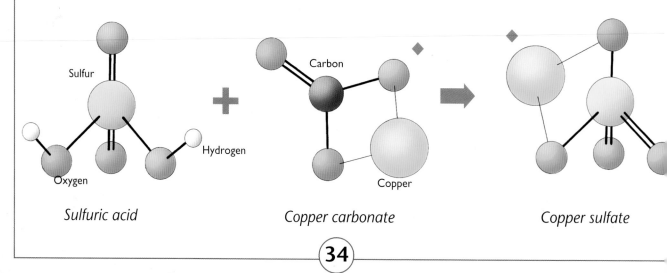

Sulfur

Hydrogen

Oxygen

Carbon

Copper

Sulfuric acid

Copper carbonate

Copper sulfate

anhydrous: a term meaning that water has been removed by heating. Many hydrated salts are crystalline. When they are heated and the water is driven off, the material changes to an anhydrous powder.

hydrate: a solid compound in crystalline form that contains molecular water. Hydrates commonly form when a solution of a soluble salt is evaporated. The water that forms part of a hydrate crystal is known as the "water of crystallization." It can usually be removed by heating, leaving an anhydrous salt.

Hydrated copper sulfate

▲▼ Hydrated copper sulfate (shown above) has been left next to a heat source. The water has been driven off to yield anhydrous copper sulfate.

Anhydrous copper sulfate

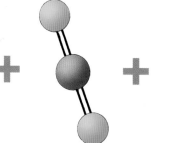

Carbon dioxide   *Water*

Reactions with copper sulfate

Copper sulfate is widely used in laboratory demonstrations. The color makes the reactions easier to see. Here are some typical reactions.

▼► Copper sulfate and ammonia solution

Ammonia solution is applied to a solution of copper sulfate using a dropper. The result is the production of copper hydroxide. Hydroxides are typically insoluble, so the copper hydroxide forms as a gelatinous precipitate.

Ammonium hydroxide solution is added to copper sulfate producing a gelatinous precipitate of copper hydroxide.

Also...

Notice that the relative proportions of reagents can make a difference to the products. In the lower part of the tube the precipitate is pale blue because a relatively large amount of copper sulfate has reacted with a relatively small amount of ammonia. By contrast, at the top of the tube the opposite is true and the solution is indigo blue. This is tetraammine copper sulfate.

The copper sulfate solution looked like this before the ammonia solution was added.

EQUATION: Copper sulfate and ammonia

Copper sulfate + ammonium solution ⇨ copper hydroxide + ammonium sulfate

$CuSO_4(aq)$ + $2NH_4OH(aq)$ ⇨ $Cu(OH)_2(aq)$ + $(NH_4)_2SO_4(aq)$

The gelatinous precipitate of copper hydroxide is redissolved as more concentrated ammonia solution is added to produce a dark blue copper compound called a "complex."

gelatinous: a term meaning made with water. Because a gelatinous precipitate is mostly water, it is of a similar density to water and will float or lie suspended in the liquid.

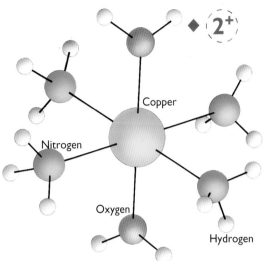

◆ 2^+

Copper

Nitrogen

Oxygen

Hydrogen

▲ A diagrammatic representation of the structure of the copper complex formed when excess ammonia solution is added to copper sulfate.

▶ Copper sulfate and hydrogen sulfide
A hydrogen sulfide solution is added to copper sulfate from a dropper. The result is a precipitate of copper sulfide. Compare this precipitate to the copper hydroxide produced in the demonstration on the opposite page.

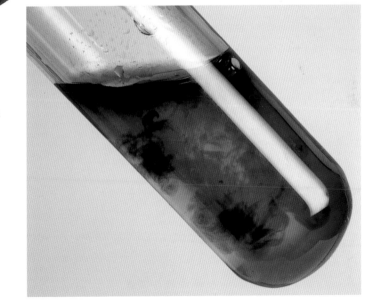

EQUATION: Copper sulfate and hydrogen sulfide

Copper sulfate + hydrogen sulfide ➪ copper sulfide + sulfuric acid

$$CuSO_4(aq) \quad + \quad H_2S(aq) \quad ➪ \quad CuS(s) \quad + \quad H_2SO_4(aq)$$

Vulcanizing rubber

Vulcanizing is the addition of sulfur to rubber. American inventor Charles Goodyear discovered the vulcanizing effect of sulfur by chance in 1839 when trying to find an improved form of rubber.

Rubber is a polymer, that is, a material made of long chains of subunits called monomers. The rubber is soft and elastic because the chains of atoms move relatively freely across each other. In the process of heating rubber with sulfur, the sulfur atoms bond with the chains of rubber, linking one chain to another. This makes it harder for the chains of rubber to move against each other, and the result is a stronger material.

Vulcanized rubber does not soften as it is heated in the way that natural rubber does and so can be used for tires and other applications in which durability and strength is important.

An extreme form of vulcanizing causes so many sulfur atoms to link together the rubber chains that the material becomes a solid. This solid is called ebonite.

▲ A vulcanized rubber hammer can be used for applying soft blows to steel panels, for example, when beating out dents from damaged vehicle bodywork.

Also...

Sulfur atoms are found in human fingernails, where they crosslink the proteins to form a rigid material. So when you look at your nails, you are looking at a natural form of vulcanizing.

monomer: a building block of a larger chain molecule ("mono" means one, "mer" means part).

polymer: a compound that is made of long chains by combining molecules (called monomers) as repeating units. ("Poly" means many, "mer" means part.)

polymerization: a chemical reaction in which large numbers of similar molecules arrange themselves into large molecules, usually long chains. This process usually happens when there is a suitable catalyst present. For example, ethylene reacts to form polyethylene in the presence of certain catalysts.

vulcanization: forming cross-links between polymer chains to increase the strength of the whole polymer. Rubbers are vulcanized using sulfur when making tires and other strong materials.

▲ A tire is a combination of layers of vulcanized rubber and textile, often incorporating steel wire. The design is for strength, durability and suppleness.

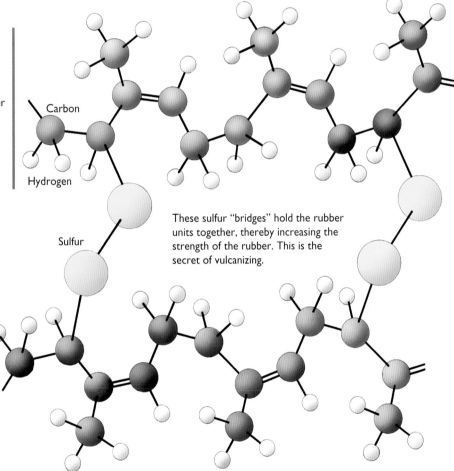

Unit of rubber

Carbon

Hydrogen

Sulfur

These sulfur "bridges" hold the rubber units together, thereby increasing the strength of the rubber. This is the secret of vulcanizing.

Unit of rubber

Foam rubber

Foam rubber contains many air bubbles to make it spongy and lightweight. Its main use is for fillings in household furniture, mattresses and carpet backing.

The latex is frothed up to incorporate air and then vulcanized in such a way that water is not evaporated from the foam before the vulcanization process is complete.

Sulfur in warfare

Sulfur can be put to many uses. Among them are the manufacture of gunpowder and poison gas.

Gunpowder is a solid mixture of sulfur, charcoal and potassium nitrate that was invented in China about one thousand years ago. It is the earliest form of explosive and is still widely used.

Sulfur reacts with chlorine to produce a yellow liquid with a revolting smell that is used in the vulcanization of rubber. This liquid has peaceful uses and is not poisonous. However, by adding more chlorine, a foul-smelling red liquid is produced. If this is in turn reacted with ethylene, it produces a gas that not only has a choking smell but is extremely poisonous. This poison gas is called mustard gas. It was used in World War I, and its effects were so horrific that it was banned by international agreement. Nevertheless, in recent years some countries have used it again, often in internal conflicts.

Mustard gas

Mustard gas (dichlorodiethyl sulfide) is a poison gas that, unfortunately, is quite easy to make and use. It is made as an oily liquid, which slowly evaporates when released into the environment.

When mustard gas is breathed into the lungs, it damages the cells on the lung lining. This causes fluid to leave the blood and fill the lungs. As a result, a person suffering from mustard gas poisoning drowns.

In less severe amounts it causes permanent lung damage and blisters on the skin. In its most characteristic form it causes blindness.

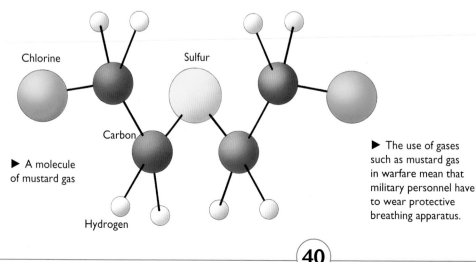

Chlorine

Sulfur

Carbon

▶ A molecule of mustard gas

Hydrogen

▶ The use of gases such as mustard gas in warfare mean that military personnel have to wear protective breathing apparatus.

explosive: a substance which, when a shock is applied to it, decomposes very rapidly, releasing a very large amount of heat and creating a large volume of gas as a shock wave.

high explosive: a form of explosive that will only work when it receives a shock from another explosive. High explosives are much more powerful than ordinary explosives. Gunpowder is not a high explosive.

poison gas: a form of gas that is used intentionally to produce widespread injury and death. (Many gases are poisonous, which is why many chemical reactions are performed in laboratory fume chambers, but they are a by-product of a reaction and not intended to cause harm.)

Gunpowder

Gunpowder is the best known and earliest form of explosive. It is made by mixing powders of sulfur, charcoal and saltpeter (potassium nitrate) together. The first people to invent gunpowder were the Chinese, and gunpowder has been in use for nearly one thousand years.

Gunpowder is ignited by means of a spark (say from tinder in a flintlock rifle), a flame (light the fuse and stand clear, as in fireworks) or an electric arc (as in detonation with an electrical plunger).

When gunpowder was first made, it was mixed and then crushed into a powder by people using hammers. As a result, from time to time, the shock of the hammers caused the powder to explode. Making gunpowder was never a good trade to be in!

The modern manufacture of gunpowder – now called black powder – is by pulverizing charcoal with sulfur and then mixing it with potassium nitrate so that the particles of nitrate, sulfur and charcoal all come into close contact. To do this, very heavy steel wheels are rolled over a black powder mixture spread on a steel plate. The mixture is then pressed into a cake and broken down into granules.

The main modern use of gunpowder is in fireworks. For this purpose the gunpowder is mixed with graphite, which coats the powder and makes it less likely to explode as it is carried around. Elsewhere, black powder is used as a first charge to set off artillery shells and other munitions.

Sulfur for life

Sulfur originally came from gases in volcanic eruptions. It is now an essential nutrient in almost all living things. Much of the sulfur in living things is recycled between generations, a process called the sulfur cycle.

Sulfur-based medicines were among the first to deal with microbial and bacterial infections and are still widely used.

The poisonous properties of some sulfur compounds are also used to help prevent infections and to preserve foods.

Preservatives

Sulfites are used widely for food preservation. They have a wide range of actions. They may kill off fungi and bacteria, preventing decay; they may stop oxygen reacting with foodstuffs, another source of decay.

Sulfites may also be used to clean vessels in which food may be placed. This is the reason, for example, that sulfite is added to water and then used to sterilize beer and wine vessels both in factories and in amateur beer and wine making.

Sulfites are also able to stop the natural decay processes that cause food to become discolored. For this reason their use has been restricted so that food cannot be stored and treated with sulfites to make it look fresher than it is.

Sulfur dioxide gas is also used as a preservative. Sulfur dioxide and sulfites both work by taking oxygen from the air and so preventing microorganisms from getting the oxygen they need to live and by creating a mildly acid environment in which organisms cannot survive.

▶ **Sulfur drugs**
Sulfur compounds have been used in the treatment of many illnesses since ancient times. For example, brimstone and molasses was a traditional "catch-all" remedy.
Modern sulfur medicines include antibacterial drugs, such as sulfa drugs. They work by destroying the enzyme that is needed for the growth of bacterial cells.

Sulfur and pesticides

A pest is any life-form that causes illness and discomfort to people or affects their food supplies or gardens.

Pesticides (named from the Latin suffix "cide," which means to kill) are chemicals that are designed to control these pests, whether they be plants or animals. From the writings of the ancient Greek Homer, we can tell that as long ago as 1000 BC, ancient civilizations were aware of the pesticide properties of sulfur.

Both the Chinese and Greeks knew about the lethal combination of sulfur and arsenic. Another of the old pesticides was Bordeaux mixture, a mixture of copper sulfate and lime. It still is used to combat fungi and to repel insects.

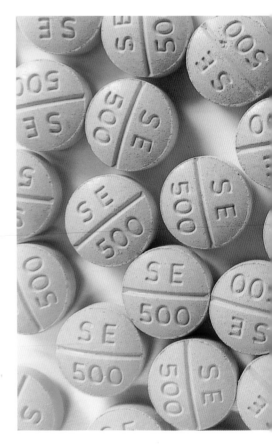

Sulfate fertilizers

Sulfates are soluble in water. This is important for plants because they need to take up their nutrients through their roots using water in the soil. Those nutrients most needed by plants to make their tissues are potassium, nitrogen and phosphorus. Sulfates are thus used as a cheap "vehicle" to carry sulfur and the other main nutrients that the plants need.

A fertilizer is produced by reacting a suitable source of potassium, nitrogen or phosphorus with sulfuric acid. About two-thirds of all the sulfuric acid made goes into the production of fertilizer.

Most fertilizers contain one or more of ammonium sulfate (nitrogen), calcium phosphate (which contains phosphorus) and sulfate of potash (potassium sulfate).

One of the best known fertilizers is called superphosphate (a combination of ammonium sulfate and phosphate), first produced by the scientist John Lawes in 1843. To make it, sulfuric acid is poured over phosphate rock, producing phosphoric acid. Ammonia gas and sulfuric acid are also reacted to produce ammonium sulfate. The two fertilizers are then mixed to make superphosphate.

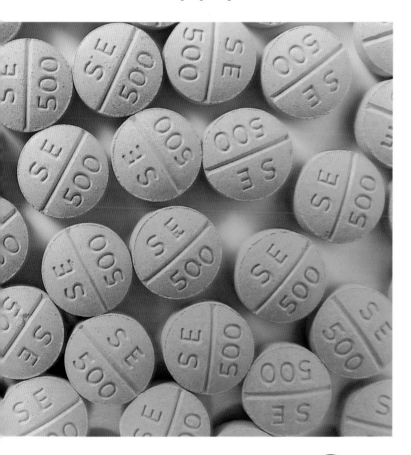

pesticide: any chemical that is designed to control pests (unwanted organisms) that are harmful to plants or animals.

preservative: a substance that prevents the natural organic decay processes from occurring. Many substances can be used safely for this purpose, including sulfites and nitrogen gas.

sulfate: a compound that includes sulfur and oxygen, for example, calcium sulfate or gypsum.

sulfide: a sulfur compound that contains no oxygen.

sulfite: a sulfur compound that contains less oxygen than a sulfate.

Energy for life

A wide range of organisms uses sulfur instead of oxygen to oxidize their energy supplies. Among the most common are bacteria.

This is why bacteria and blue-green algae are able to live in places with very little oxygen. The vastness of the deep ocean waters is one example, the areas near geysers and volcanoes are another.

Whereas green plants give off oxygen, organisms that live in oxygen-poor water give off sulfur as part of their living processes. These organisms get all the energy they need by fermenting dead tissue using sulfur-containing compounds.

Also...

In recent years farmers near industrial regions have noticed that their yields of cereals have declined almost in proportion to the rate at which sulfur has been removed from the smokestacks of power stations. This is because plants have been using the sulfur in the acid rain as a fertilizer. Now acid rain has been reduced, farmers are having to increase their applications of sulfate fertilizers in order to maintain their yields!

Key facts about...
Sulfur

Has no taste

Has no smell

Poor conductor of electricity and heat

Can be found as native sulfur in crystalline form

A very reactive element that combines with almost all other elements

A mustard-yellow solid, chemical symbol S

Melts at 119°C, just a little over the boiling point of water

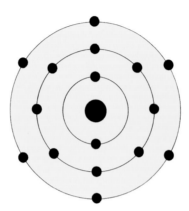

Soft and can be scratched with a fingernail

Density 2 g/ml, about twice that of water

Insoluble in water

Atomic number 16, atomic weight about 32

SHELL DIAGRAMS
The shell diagram on this page is a representation of an atom of the element sulfur. The total number of electrons is shown in the relevant orbitals, or shells, around the central nucleus.

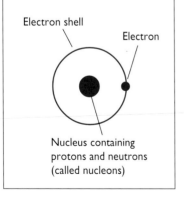

Electron shell

Electron

Nucleus containing protons and neutrons (called nucleons)

▶ A hydrogen sulfide solution is added to silver nitrate, leaving a dark brown precipitate of silver sulfide. Sulfide precipitates are mostly a dark color and are frequently black.

▼ "Crash cooling" molten sulfur causes the atoms to form long chains and the sulfur forms a plasticlike substance that turns brittle as the atoms assume a more stable structure (see pages 6 and 7 for more about this demonstration).

The Periodic Table

The Periodic Table sets out the relationships among the elements of the Universe. According to the Periodic Table, certain elements fall into groups. The pattern of these groups has, in the past, allowed scientists to predict elements that had not at that time been discovered. It can still be used today to predict the properties of unfamiliar elements.

The Periodic Table was first described by a Russian teacher, Dmitry Ivanovich Mendeleev, between 1869 and 1870. He was interested in writing a chemistry textbook and wanted to show his students that there were certain patterns in the elements that had been discovered. So he set out the elements (of which there were 57 at the time) according to their known properties. On the assumption that there was pattern to the elements, he left blank spaces where elements seemed to be missing. Using this first version of the Periodic Table, he was able to predict in detail the chemical and physical properties of elements that had not yet been discovered. Other scientists began to look for the missing elements, and they soon found them.

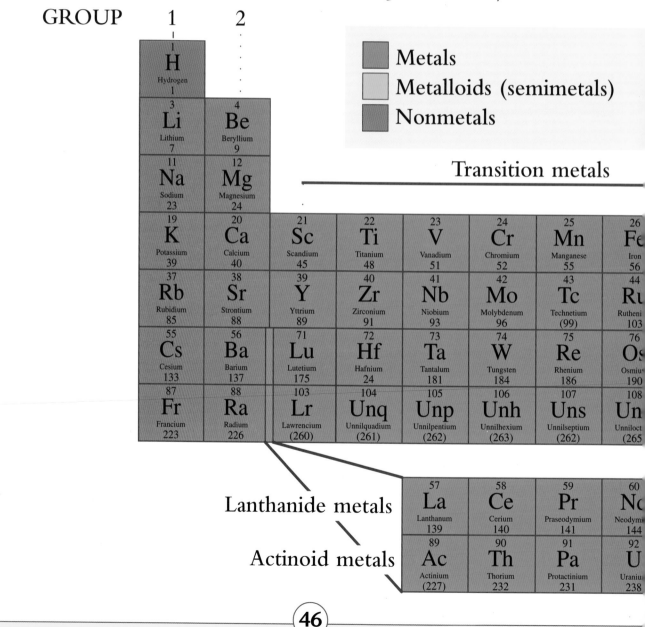

Hydrogen did not seem to fit into the table, and so he placed it in a box on its own. Otherwise the elements were all placed horizontally. When an element was reached with properties similar to the first one in the top row, a second row was started. By following this rule, similarities among the elements can be found by reading up and down. By reading across the rows, the elements progressively increase their atomic number. This number indicates the number of positively charged particles (protons) in the nucleus of each atom. This is also the number of negatively charged particles (electrons) in the atom.

The chemical properties of an element depend on the number of electrons in the outermost shell.

Atoms can form compounds by sharing electrons in their outermost shells. This explains why atoms with a full set of electrons (like helium, an inert gas) are unreactive, whereas atoms with an incomplete electron shell (such as chlorine) are very reactive. Elements can also combine by the complete transfer of electrons from metals to nonmetals, and the compounds formed contain ions.

Radioactive elements lose particles from their nucleus and electrons from their surrounding shells. As a result they change their atomic number and so become new elements.

Key:

Atomic (proton) number

13
Al — Symbol
Aluminum
27 — Name

Approximate relative atomic mass

3	4	5	6	7	0
					2 **He** Helium 4
5 **B** Boron 11	6 **C** Carbon 12	7 **N** Nitrogen 14	8 **O** Oxygen 16	9 **F** Fluorine 19	10 **Ne** Neon 20
13 **Al** Aluminum 27	14 **Si** Silicon 28	15 **P** Phosphorus 31	16 **S** Sulfur 32	17 **Cl** Chlorine 35	18 **Ar** Argon 40
31 **Ga** Gallium 70	32 **Ge** Germanium 73	33 **As** Arsenic 75	34 **Se** Selenium 79	35 **Br** Bromine 80	36 **Kr** Krypton 84
49 **In** Indium 115	50 **Sn** Tin 119	51 **Sb** Antimony 122	52 **Te** Tellurium 128	53 **I** Iodine 127	54 **Xe** Xenon 131
81 **Tl** Thallium 204	82 **Pb** Lead 207	83 **Bi** Bismuth 209	84 **Po** Polonium (209)	85 **At** Astatine (210)	86 **Rn** Radon (222)

Transition metals (partial, left edge):

27 **Co** Cobalt 59	28 **Ni** Nickel 59	29 **Cu** Copper 64	30 **Zn** Zinc 65
45 **Rh** Rhodium 103	46 **Pd** Palladium 106	47 **Ag** Silver 108	48 **Cd** Cadmium 112
77 **Ir** Iridium 192	78 **Pt** Platinum 195	79 **Au** Gold 197	80 **Hg** Mercury 201
109 **Une** Unnilennium (266)			

Lanthanides/Actinides (partial):

61 **Pm** Promethium (145)	62 **Sm** Samarium 150	63 **Eu** Europium 152	64 **Gd** Gadolinium 157	65 **Tb** Terbium 159	66 **Dy** Dysprosium 163	67 **Ho** Holmium 165	68 **Er** Erbium 167	69 **Tm** Thulium 169	70 **Yb** Ytterbium 173
93 **Np** Neptunium (237)	94 **Pu** Plutonium (244)	95 **Am** Americium (243)	96 **Cm** Curium (247)	97 **Bk** Berkelium (247)	98 **Cf** Californium (251)	99 **Es** Einsteinium (252)	100 **Fm** Fermium (257)	101 **Md** Mendelevium (258)	102 **No** Nobelium (259)

Understanding equations

As you read through this book, you will notice that many pages contain equations using symbols. If you are not familiar with these symbols, read this page. Symbols make it easy for chemists to write out the reactions that are occurring in a way that allows a better understanding of the processes involved.

Symbols for the elements

The basis of the modern use of symbols for elements dates back to the 19th century. At this time a shorthand was developed using the first letter of the element wherever possible. Thus "O" stands for oxygen, "H" stands for hydrogen and so on. However, if we were to use only the first letter, then there could be some confusion. For example, nitrogen and nickel would both use the symbols N. To overcome this problem, many elements are symbolized using the first two letters of their full name, and the second letter is not in capitals. Thus although nitrogen is N, nickel becomes Ni. Not all symbols come from the English name; many use the Latin name instead. This is why, for example, gold is not G but Au (for the Latin *aurum*) and sodium has the symbol Na, from the Latin *natrium*.

Compounds of elements are made by combining letters. Thus the molecule carbon

Written and symbolic equations
In this book important chemical equations are briefly stated in words (these are called word equations) and are then shown in their symbolic form along with the states.

What reaction the equation illustrates

Written equation

Symbol equation

EQUATION: The formation of calcium hydroxide

Calcium oxide + water ⇨ calcium hydroxide

$$CaO(s) \quad + \quad H_2O(l) \quad ⇨ \quad Ca(OH)_2(aq)$$
heated

Sometimes you will find an additional description below the symbolic equation.

Symbol showing the state: *s* is for solid, *l* is for liquid, *g* is for gas and *aq* is for aqueous.

Diagrams
Some of the equations are shown as graphic representations.

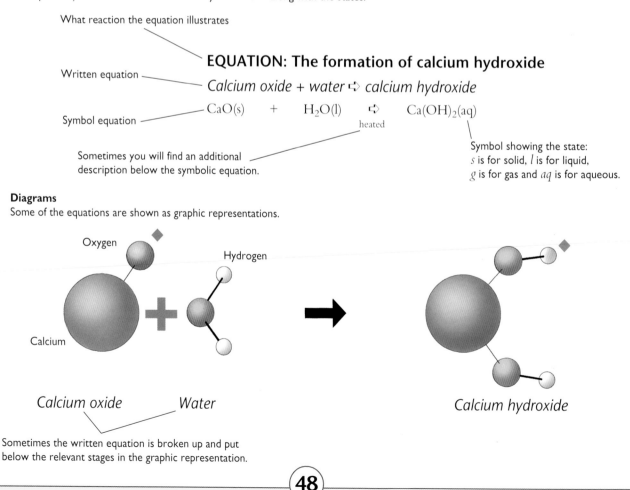

Oxygen

Hydrogen

Calcium

Calcium oxide   *Water*

Calcium hydroxide

Sometimes the written equation is broken up and put below the relevant stages in the graphic representation.

monoxide is CO. By using letters that are not capitals for the second letter of an element, it is possible to show that cobalt, symbol Co, is not the same as the molecule carbon monoxide, CO.

However, the letters can be made to do much more than this. In many molecules, atoms combine in unequal numbers. So, for example, carbon dioxide has one atom of carbon for every two of oxygen. This is shown by using the number 2 beside the oxygen, and the symbol becomes CO_2.

In practice, some groups of atoms combine as a unit with other substances. Thus, for example, calcium bicarbonate (one of the compounds used in some antacid pills) is written $Ca(HCO_3)_2$. This shows that the part of the substance inside the brackets reacts as a unit, and the "2" outside the brackets shows the presence of two such units.

Some substances attract water molecules to themselves. To show this a dot is used. Thus the blue-colored form of copper sulfate is written $CuSO_4.5H_2O$. In this case five molecules of water attract to one copper sulfate. When you see the dot, you know that this water can be driven off by heating; it is part of the crystal structure.

In a reaction substances change by rearranging the combinations of atoms. The way they change is shown by using the chemical symbols, placing those that will react (the starting materials, or reactants) on the left and the products of the reaction on the right. Between the two, chemists use an arrow to show which way the reaction is occurring.

It is possible to describe a reaction in words. This gives a word equation. Word equations are used throughout this book. However, it is easier to understand what is happening by using an equation containing symbols. These are also given in many places. They are not used when the equations are very complex.

In any equation both sides balance; that is, there must be an equal number of like atoms on both sides of the arrow. When you try to write down reactions, you, too, must balance your equation; you cannot have a few atoms left over at the end!

The symbols in brackets are abbreviations for the physical state of each substance taking part, so that (s) is used for solid, (l) for liquid, (g) for gas and (aq) for an aqueous solution, that is, a solution of a substance dissolved in water.

Atoms and ions
Each sphere represents a particle of an element. A particle can be an atom or an ion. Each atom or ion is associated with other atoms or ions through bonds – forces of attraction. The size of the particles and the nature of the bonds can be extremely important in determining the nature of the reaction or the properties of the compound.

Chemical symbols, equations and diagrams
The arrangement of any molecule or compound can be shown in one of the two ways below, depending on which gives the clearer picture. The left-hand diagram is called a ball-and-stick diagram because it uses rods and spheres to show the structure of the material. This example shows water, H_2O. There are two hydrogen atoms and one oxygen atom.

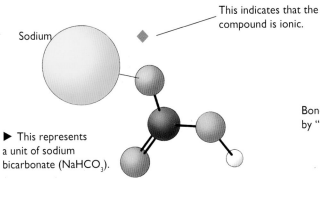

Sodium

This indicates that the compound is ionic.

▶ This represents a unit of sodium bicarbonate ($NaHCO_3$).

Bond shown by "stick"

The term "unit" is sometimes used to simplify the representation of a combination of ions.

Colors too
The colors of each of the particles help differentiate the elements involved. The diagram can then be matched to the written and symbolic equation given with the diagram. In the case above, oxygen is red and hydrogen is gray.

Glossary of technical terms

acid: compounds containing hydrogen that can attack and dissolve many substances. Acids are described as weak or strong, dilute or concentrated, mineral or organic.

acidity: a general term for the strength of an acid in a solution.

anhydrous: a term meaning that water has been removed by heating. Many hydrated salts are crystalline. When they are heated and the water is driven off, the material changes to an anhydrous powder.

catalyst: a substance that speeds up a chemical reaction but itself remains unaltered at the end of the reaction.

combustion: the special case of oxidization of a substance in which a considerable amount of heat and usually light are given out. Combustion is often referred to as "burning."

corrosive: a substance, either an acid or an alkali, that *rapidly* attacks a wide range of other substances.

crystal systems: there are seven patterns or systems into which all of the world's crystals can be grouped. They are: cubic, hexagonal, rhombohedral, tetragonal, orthorhombic, monoclinic and triclinic.

cubic crystal system: groupings of crystals that look like cubes.

electrode: a conductor that forms one terminal of a cell.

electrolyte: a solution that conducts electricity.

explosive: a substance which, when a shock is applied to it, decomposes very rapidly, releasing a very large amount of heat and creating a large volume of gas as a shock wave.

flux: a material used to make it easier for a liquid to flow. A flux dissolves metal oxides and so prevents a metal from oxidizing while being heated.

gelatinous: a term meaning made with water. Because a gelatinous precipitate is mostly water, it is of a similar density to water and will float or lie suspended in the liquid.

high explosive: a form of explosive that will only work when it receives a shock from another explosive. High explosives are much more powerful than ordinary explosives. Gunpowder is not a high explosive.

hydrate: a solid compound in crystalline form that contains molecular water. Hydrates commonly form when a solution of a soluble salt is evaporated. The water that forms part of a hydrate crystal is known as the "water of crystallization." It can usually be removed by heating, leaving an anhydrous salt.

hydrothermal: a process in which hot water is involved. It is usually used in the context of rock formation because hot water and other fluids sent outward from liquid magmas are important carriers of metals and the minerals that form gemstones.

ion: an atom, or group of atoms, that has gained or lost one or more electrons and so developed an electrical charge. Ions behave differently from electrically neutral atoms and molecules. They can move in an electric field, and they can also bind strongly to solvent molecules such as water. Positively charged ions are called cations; negatively charged ions are called anions. Ions can carry an electrical current through solutions.

latent heat: the amount of heat that is absorbed or released during the process of changing state between gas, liquid or solid. For example, heat is absorbed when a substance melts and it is released again when the substance solidifies.

melting point: the temperature at which a substance changes state from a solid to a liquid. It is the same as freezing point.

mineral acid: an acid that does not contain carbon and which attacks minerals. Hydrochloric, sulfuric and nitric acids are the main mineral acids.

monoclinic system: a grouping of crystals that look like double-ended chisel blades.

monomer: a building block of a larger chain molecule ("mono" means one, "mer" means part).

ore: a rock containing enough of a useful substance to make mining it worthwhile.

oxidizing agent: a substance that removes electrons from another substance (and therefore is itself reduced).

pesticide: any chemical that is designed to control pests (unwanted organisms) that are harmful to plants or animals.

poison gas: a form of gas that is used intentionally to produce widespread injury and death. (Many gases are poisonous, which is why many chemical reactions are performed in laboratory fume chambers, but they are a by-product of a reaction and not intended to cause harm.)

polymer: a compound that is made of long chains by combining molecules (called monomers) as repeating units. ("Poly" means many, "mer" means part.)

polymerization: a chemical reaction in which large numbers of similar molecules arrange themselves into large molecules, usually long chains. This process usually happens when

there is a suitable catalyst present. For example, ethylene reacts to form polyethylene in the presence of certain catalysts.

preservative: a substance that prevents the natural organic decay processes from occurring. Many substances can be used safely for this purpose, including sulfites and nitrogen gas.

pyrite: "mineral of fire." This name comes from the fact that pyrite (iron sulfide) will give off sparks if struck with a stone.

reducing agent: a substance that gives electrons to another substance. Carbon monoxide is a reducing agent when passed over copper oxide, turning it to copper and producing carbon dioxide gas. Similarly, iron oxide is reduced to iron in a blast furnace. Sulfur dioxide is a reducing agent used for bleaching bread.

saturated: a state in which a liquid can hold no more of a substance. If any more of the substance is added, it will not dissolve.

saturated solution: a solution that holds the maximum possible amount of dissolved material. The amount of material in solution varies with the temperature; cold solutions can hold less dissolved solid material than hot solutions. Gases are more soluble in cold liquids than hot liquids.

smoke: a mixture of both small solids and gases.

strong acid: an acid that has completely dissociated (ionized) in water. Mineral acids are strong acids.

sulfate: a compound that includes sulfur and oxygen, for example, calcium sulfate or gypsum.

sulfide: a sulfur compound that contains no oxygen.

sulfite: a sulfur compound that contains less oxygen than a sulfate.

viscous: slow-moving, syrupy. A liquid that has a low viscosity is said to be mobile.

vulcanization: forming cross-links between polymer chains to increase the strength of the whole polymer. Rubbers are vulcanized using sulfur when making tires and other strong materials.

weak acid: an acid that has only partly dissociated (ionized) in water. Most organic acids are weak acids.

Master Index

A

A-bomb **15:** 38
acetate **8:** 41
acetic acid **1:** 31, **7:** 33, **8:** 29
acetone **7:** 34, **8:** 28
acetylene **8:** 29, **14:** 22
acid **1:** 12, 18, 19, 20, 22, 23, 34, 35, 36, 37, **2:** 31, **3:** 12, 21, 29, 39, 42, **7:** 14, 33, **13:** 19, 26, 27
acid burn **1:** 24, **13:** 26, **2:** 32, 33, **3:** 13, **4:** 10, **7:** 40, 42, 43, **10:** 12, **11:** 31, 32, **12:** 13, 29, 42, **13:** 18, 19, 22, 23
acidity **1:** 20–21
acidosis **1:** 28
acids **9:** 11
acid soil **4:** 17
activated charcoal **8:** 22, 23, **14:** 27
addition polymer **8:** 32–35
adhesive **3:** 22, 23, **12:** 20
adsorption **14:** 27, **7:** 35, **8:** 23
aeration **12:** 8, 9
aeroembolism **11:** 37
Ag **5:** 5, 44
agate **9:** 13, 14
Agent Orange **14:** 29
air **11:** 38, **12:** 6, 7, 17
air bag **11:** 29
Al **7:** 4, 44
alchemists, alchemy **1:** 22, 23, **15:** 11
alclad **7:** 23
alcohols **8:** 28
algae **3:** 4, 40, **11:** 43
algal blooms **11:** 43
alkali **1:** 20, 34, 35, **2:** 5, 32, **7:** 14, 33, 36, **11:** 12, 14, 15, 39
alkaline **1:** 20, 32, 33, **2:** 6, 31, 32
alkalies (paraffins) **8:** 28
alkanes (paraffins) **8:** 28
alloy **4:** 34, 35, 36–37, 40, **5:** 20, **6:** 20, 22, 41, **7:** 22–23, **9:** 31, **10:** 40, 41
alpha particle **15:** 8, 42
alpha radiation **15:** 8, 9
alum **7:** 4, 7, 36, **8:** 15
alumina **7:** 16, 17, 18, 19, 34
alumina–silica gel **8:** 27, **1:** 26, 36
aluminum **1:** 26, 36, **2:** 32, **4:** 22, 23, **5:** 21, 35, **7:** 4, 44, **6:** 22, **9:** 11, 20, 26, 34, 37, **10:** 39, **11:** 37, **12:** 10, 38, **15:** 9
aluminum foil **7:** 21, 30
aluminum hydroxide **7:** 36, 37, 38
aluminum oxide **7:** 7, 14, 16, 17, 18, 34, 35, **8:** 20, 21, **9:** 13, **12:** 11, 39, **4:** 17
aluminum silicate **9:** 26
aluminum sulfate **7:** 7, 36, 38, **8:** 15
amalgam **5:** 35, 42, **6:** 26, 36, 37, **7:** 22, **14:** 19
amalgamation **5:** 39
Amatol **11:** 27
amethyst **9:** 12
amino acids **8:** 36
ammonia **1:** 16–17, 22, 26, 27, 32, **2:** 28, 29, **7:** 36, **11:** 12–17, 36, 37, **13:** 36, 43, **14:** 17, 34, 39
ammonia fountain **11:** 15
ammonia solution **5:** 27

ammonite **3:** 9
ammonium chloride **1:** 22, 23, **2:** 28, 29, **4:** 41, **6:** 14, 15, **11:** 13, **14:** 34
ammonium dichromate **11:** 24, 25
ammonium hydroxide **11:** 12
ammonium nitrate **11:** 13, 27
ammonium nitrite **11:** 27
ammonium perchlorate **12:** 39, **14:** 24
ammonium sulfate **7:** 36, **11:** 14, **13:** 43
ammunition **10:** 15, **11:** 27
amorphous **9:** 38
amphiboles **9:** 24
amphoteric **6:** 10, **7:** 14
anesthetics **14:** 5
anglesite **10:** 7
anhydrous **13:** 34
anions **3:** 29, **6:** 12,
annealing **7:** 20, **9:** 41
anode **2:** 23, 26, **3:** 37, **6:** 12, 13, **7:** 19, 25, **10:** 11
anodizing **7:** 26
antacid **2:** 31, **3:** 5, 42, 49, **8:** 15
anthracite **8:** 7
antibacterial agent **6:** 38
antimony **10:** 15, 40
antimony-133 **15:** 29
antioxidant **11:** 10
antiseptic **14:** 41
apatite **11:** 42
aqua fortis **1:** 26, **11:** 36
aqua regia **1:** 22, 26, **5:** 41, **11:** 36
aquamarine **9:** 23, **12:** 10
aquifers **2:** 20
Ar **1:** 5, 44
architectural brass **5:** 19
argon **1:** 38, 39, 42, 45, **4:** 30, **11:** 8, 9, **12:** 17, **15:** 11
arsenic **2:** 30, **13:** 42
asbestos **14:** 20
asphalt **8:** 26, 27
aspirin **1:** 30
atmosphere **3:** 12, **11:** 6, **12:** 6, 8, 12
atom **1:** 4, 38, **15:** 4, 7
atomic bomb **15:** 38, 39
atomic number **1–15:** 44, 45, 47
atomic weight **1–15:** 44, 45, 47
atoms **8:** 8
Au **5:** 5, 45
augite **9:** 24
aurora **12:** 7, **11:** 7
Australia **7:** 11
azide **11:** 29

B

background radiation **15:** 14–15
Bacon, Roger **11:** 26
bacteria **13:** 8, 20
Baekland, Leo **8:** 31
Bakelite **8:** 31
baking powder **2:** 30
baking soda **2:** 28, 30, **8:** 14
barite **13:** 12
barium chlorate **14:** 24
barium-142 **15:** 28
barium peroxide **4:** 22
barium sulfate **13:** 12

barometer **6:** 30
basalt **9:** 24, 43, **15:** 18
base **1:** 22, 23, 32–33, 34, **2:** 32, **3:** 21, 25
base bullion **10:** 10
basic-oxygen furnace process **4:** 30, 31
basic-oxygen process **12:** 27
battery **4:** 41, **6:** 5, 12, **10:** 28, **13:** 30, 31
bauxite **7:** 10–11, 13, 14, 16, 18
Bayer, Karl oseph **7:** 12
Bayer process **7:** 14, 16
becquerel **15:** 13, 22
Becquerel, A. H. **6:** 35, **15:** 5, 12, 22
bell-making bronze **5:** 21
bends **11:** 7
Benin bronze **5:** 19
benzene ring **8:** 33
beryl **7:** 8, **9:** 22
beryllium **7:** 8, **9:** 22
Bessemer Converter **4:** 31, **12:** 27
Bessemer, Sir Henry **4:** 31
beta particle **15:** 8
beta radiation **15:** 8, 9
bicarbonate **1:** 29, 31
Big Bang **15:** 7
biotite **7:** 6, **9:** 26
bismuth **10:** 11
black phosphorus **11:** 38
blast furnace **4:** 24, 25, 26, 27, **12:** 26
bleach **4:** 42, **12:** 21, **13:** 18, 20–21, **14:** 14, 15, 24
bleaching agent **13:** 18–21
blood **12:** 15
blood (salts) **2:** 18, 19
blue–green algae **11:** 18, 19, 22
Blue John **14:** 8, 36
blue vitriol **5:** 24, **13:** 32
body **2:** 18,19, **3:** 5, 32
bog iron ore **4:** 13
bond **1:** 9, 11, **2:** 23, **3:** 49
bone **3:** 5, 32
Bordeaux mixture **5:** 23, **13:** 34, 42
bornite **5:** 6
boron oxide **9:** 38
borosilicate glass **9:** 39
Br **14:** 5, 45
brass **5:** 18–19, 20, 27, **6:** 4, 20, **10:** 15
braze **5:** 18, **7:** 20
Brazil **7:** 11
breeder reactor **15:** 35
brimstone **13:** 4, 5, 10
brimstone and treacle **13:** 42
brine **1:** 14, 15, **2:** 12, 13, 25, 26, 27, 28, 29, 40, **6:** 33, **14:** 18, 19, 20
bromide **14:** 4
bromine **8:** 23, **14:** 4, 5, 6, 8, 27, 42–43, 45
bromothymol blue **1:** 21
bronze **5:** 20–21, 27, 34, **6:** 20, 21, **10:** 40, 41
Bronze Age **5:** 20, **10:** 5, 41
bronze coins **10:** 44
buckled ring **13:** 6
buckminsterfullerene **8:** 8, 22
buffer **1:** 28, 29
building stone **3:** 18

burette **1:** 35
burnt lime **3:** 22
burnt ocher **4:** 13
butane **8:** 7, 26, 28

C

C **8:** 4, 44
Ca **3:** 4, 44
cadmium **6:** 5, 40–43, 45, **15:** 34
cadmium battery **6:** 41
cadmium borate **6:** 42
cadmium hydroxide **6:** 41
cadmium plating **6:** 40
cadmium sulfide **6:** 40, 42, 43, **9:** 41, **13:** 12, 24, 25
cadmium telluride **6:** 42
cadmium test **6:** 40
calcite **3:** 8, 10, 14, 16, 33, **9:** 18
calcium **3:** 4, 6, 38, 40, 42, 44, **7:** 6, **9:** 11, 20, 38,
calcium bicarbonate **1:** 29, **3:** 15, 27, 38, 42
calcium carbonate **1:** 23, 29, 34, **3:** 4, 8, 12, 15, 16, 21, 26, 33, 39, 43, **4:** 31, **8:** 15, **9:** 9, 18, 39, 40, **14:** 35
calcium chlorate **14:** 14, 16, 24
calcium chloride **2:** 28, **14:** 19
calcium fluoride **3:** 8, **14:** 8, 9
calcium hydrogen carbonate **3:** 38
calcium hydroxide **3:** 6, 24, 26, 28, **11:** 14
calcium ions **3:** 25, 28, 40,
calcium oxide **2:** 29, **3:** 20, 24, 48, **4:** 26, 31, **7:** 16, **11:** 14, **12:** 26, **14:** 14
calcium phosphate **3:** 32, **11:** 38, 42, 43, **14:** 37
calcium silicate **4:** 26
calcium sulfate **3:** 8, 30, **4:** 25, **13:** 9, 12, 13, 32, **11:** 43
calomel **6:** 32
camphor **8:** 31
cancer **15:** 42
cans **7:** 32, 33, 40
carats **5:** 40
carbohydrate **8:** 18
carbon **1:** 24, **4:** 27, 28, 29, 30, 31, 32, 34, 41, **6:** 14, 15, **7:** 18, 19, **8:** 4, 44, **9:** 13, **10:** 8, 10, **12:** 24, 26, **13:** 26, 27, **14:** 13, 15, **15:** 7
carbon black **4:** 41, **8:** 22
carbon compounds **8:** 6
carbon cycle **8:** 10–11, 13
carbon dating **15:** 18
carbon dioxide **1:** 23, 28, **2:** 28, 29, 30, 31, **3:** 12, 19, 26, 43, 49, **4:** 26, 27, **7:** 38, 39, **8:** 10, 11, 12–15, 18, **11:** 8, **12:** 14, 15, 24, 38, 41
carbon dioxide, radioactive **15:** 14
carbon-14 **11:** 6, **15:** 7, 10, 16, 17, 19
carbonic acid **1:** 28–29, **3:** 12
Carboniferous Period **8:** 7
carbon monoxide **4:** 24, 27, 30, **5:** 8, 9, **6:** 8, **8:** 16–17, **10:** 8, **12:** 13, 24

D

E

F

MAR 1 8 1998